John Moore

A view of society and manners in France, Switzerland, and Germany

With anecdotes relating to some eminent characters. Vol. 2

John Moore

A view of society and manners in France, Switzerland, and Germany
With anecdotes relating to some eminent characters. Vol. 2

ISBN/EAN: 9783337150389

Printed in Europe, USA, Canada, Australia, Japan

Cover: Foto ©Suzi / pixelio.de

More available books at **www.hansebooks.com**

A

V I E W

O F

SOCIETY and MANNERS

I N

FRANCE, SWITZERLAND, AND GERMANY:

W I T H

ANECDOTES relating to fome EMINENT CHARACTERS·

BY JOHN MOORE, M.D.

VOL. II.

Strenua nos exercet inertia: navibus atque
Quadrigis petimus bene vivere. Quod petis, hic eft.
Hor.

The SIXTH EDITION, Correfted.

LONDON:
Printed for A. Strahan; and T. Cadell, in the Strand.
MDCCLXXXVI.

CONTENTS

OF THE

SECOND VOLUME.

A 2

A 3

5

A VIEW

A

V I E W

OF

SOCIETY AND MANNERS

IN

France, Switzerland, and Germany.

L E T T E R L.

DEAR SIR,   Frankfort.

SINCE my return from Darmſtadt, the weather has been ſo very bad, that I have paſſed the time moſtly at home. That I may obey your injunctions to write regularly at the ſtated periods, I will ſend you the ſubſtance of a converſation I had within theſe few days with a foreigner, a man of letters, with

VOL. II.   B   whom

whom I am in a confiderable degree of intimacy.

This gentleman has never been in England, but he fpeaks the language a little,
underftands it very well, and has ftudied
many of our beft Authors. He faid,
that he had found in fome Englifh books,
a folidity of reafoning, and a ftrength of
expreffion, fuperior to any thing he had
met with elfewhere;—that the Englifh
hiftory furnifhed examples of patriotifm
and zeal for civil liberty, equal to what
was recorded in the Greek or Roman
ftory;—that Englifh poetry difplayed a
fublimity of thought, and a knowledge of
the human heart, which no writings, ancient or modern, could furpafs; and in
philofophy it was pretty generally allowed,
that the Englifh nation had no rival.—He
then mentioned the improvements made by
Englifhmen in medicine and other arts,
their fuperiority in navigation, commerce,
and manufactures; and even hinted fome-
                                    thing

thing in praife of a few Englifh ftatefmen.
He concluded his panegyric by faying,
that thefe confiderations had given him the
higheft idea of the Englifh nation, and had
led him to 'cultivate the acquaintance of
many Englifhmen whom he had occafionally met on their travels. But he frankly
acknowledged, that his connection with
thefe, had not contributed to fupport the
idea he had formed of their nation.

As I had heard fentiments of the fame
kind infinuated by others, I replied at fome
length, obferving, that if he had lived in
the moft brilliant period of Roman grandeur, and had accidentally met with a few
Romans in Greece or Afia, and had formed
his opinion of that illuftrious common-
wealth from the conduct and converfation
of thefe travellers, his ideas would, in all
probability, have been very different from
thofe which the writings of Livy, Cæfar,
Cicero, and Virgil, had given him of the
Roman people:—That the manners and

behaviour

behaviour of the few Englifh he might have met abroad, fo far from giving him a juft view of the character of the whole nation, very poffibly had led him to falfe conclufions with regard to the character of thofe very individuals. For that I myfelf had known many young Englifhmen, who, after having led a diffipated, infignificant kind of life while on their travels, and while the natural objects of their ambition were at a diftance, had changed their conduct entirely upon their return, applied to bufinefs as eagerly as they had formerly launched into extravagance, and had at length become very ufeful members of the community.

But, continued I, throwing this confideration out of the queftion, the real character of a people can only be difcovered by living among them on a familiar footing, and for a confiderable time. This is neceffary before we can form a juft idea of any nation; but perhaps more fo with

refpect

refpect to the Englifh, than any other : for in no nation are the education, fentiments, and purfuits of thofe who travel, fo different from thofe of the people who remain at home.

The firft clafs is compofed of a few invalids, a great many young men raw from the univerfity, and fome idle men of fortune, void of ambition, and incapable of application, who, every now and then, faunter through Europe, becaufe they know not how to employ their time at home.

The fecond clafs is made up of younger brothers, who are bred to the army, navy, the law, and other profeffions;—all who follow commerce, are employed in manufactures, or farming;—and, in one word, all who, not being born to independent fortunes, endeavour to remedy that inconveniency by induftry, and the cultivation of their talents.

B 3   England

England is the only country in Europe whofe inhabitants never leave it in fearch of fortune. There are, moderately fpeaking, twenty Frenchmen in London for every Englifhman at Paris. By far the greater part of thofe Frenchmen travel to get money, and almoft all the Englifh to fpend it. But we fhould certainly be led into great errors, by forming an idea of the character of the French nation from that of the French fiddlers, dancing-maf- ters, dentifts, and valet-de-chambres to be met with in England, or other parts of Europe.

The gentleman acknowledged, that it would be unfair to decide on the French character from that of their fiddlers and dancing-mafters; but added, that he did not perceive that the Englifh could rea- fonably complain, fhould foreigners form an opinion of their national character from the men of fortune, rank, and the moft liberal education of their ifland.

I an-

I anſwered, they certainly would, becauſe young men of high rank and great fortune carry a ſet of ideas along with them from their infancy, which very often diſappoint the purpoſes of the beſt education.——Let a child of high rank be brought up with all the care and attention the moſt judi-cious parents and maſters can give;—let him be told, that perſonal qualities alone can make him truly reſpectable;—that the fortuitous circumſtances of birth and for-tune afford no juſt foundation for eſteem; —that knowledge and virtue are the true ſources of honour and happineſs;—that idleneſs produces vice and miſery;—that without application he cannot acquire know-ledge;—and that without knowledge he will dwindle into inſignificance, in ſpite of rank and fortune :——Let theſe things be inculcated with all the power of per-ſuaſion; let them be illuſtrated by example, and inſinuated by fable and allegory;— yet, do we not daily ſee the effect of all this

counteracted by the infinuations of fervants
and bafe fycophants, who give an importance to far different. qualities, and preach
a much more agreeable doctrine ?———

They make eternal allufions in all their
difcourfe and behaviour to the great eftate
the young fpark is one day to have, and the
great man he muft be, independent of any
effort of his own. They plainly infinuate,
if they do not directly fay it, that ftudy and
application, tho' proper enough for hofpital
boys, is unneceffary, or perhaps unbecoming
a man of fafhion. They talk with rapture
of the hounds, hunters, and race-horfes of
one great man; of the rich liveries and
brilliant equipage of another; and extol,
above all others, thofe who poffefs that firft
of virtues, liberality to their fervants. They
tell their young mafter, that his rank and
eftate entitle him to have finer hounds,
horfes, liveries, and equipage than either,
and to be more liberal to his fervants; and
confequently a greater man in every refpect.
                                        This

This kind of poifon, being often poured upon the young fprouts of fortune and quality, gradually blafts the vigour of the plants, and renders all care and cultivation ineffectual.

If we fuppofe that domeftics of another character could be placed about a boy of high rank, and every meafure taken to infpire him with other fentiments; he cannot ftir abroad, he cannot go into company without perceiving his own importance, and the attention that is paid to him. His childifh pranks are called fpirited actions; his pert fpeeches are converted into bon mots; and when reproved or punifhed by his parent or mafter, ten to one but fome obfequious intermeddler will tell him that he has fuffered great injuftice.

The youth, improving all this to the purpofes of indolence and vanity, arrives at length at the comfortable perfuafion, that ftudy or application of any kind would in

him

him be fuperfluous ;—that he ought only
to feek amufement, for, at the bleffed age
of twenty-one, diftinction, deference, admiration, and all other good things will be
added unto him.

A young man, on the other hand, who
is born to no fuch expectations, has no fycophants around him to pervert his underftanding ;—when he behaves improperly,
he inftantly fees the marks of difapprobation
on every countenance :—He daily meets
with people who inform him of his faults
without ceremony or circumlocution.—He
perceives that nobody cares for his bad humour or caprice, and very naturally concludes that he had beft correct his temper.
—He finds that he is apt to be neglected in
company, and that the only remedy for this
inconveniency will be the rendering himfelf
agreeable.—He loves affluence, diftinction,
and admiration, as well as the rich and
great ; but becomes fully convinced that he
can never obtain even the fhadow of them,
                                                  otherwife

otherwife than by ufeful and ornamental acquirements. The truth of thofe precepts, which is proved by rhetoric and fyllogifm to the boy of fortune, is *experimentally* felt by him who has no fortune; and the difference which this makes is infinite.

So that the fon of a gentleman of moderate fortune has a probability of knowing more of the world at the age of fixteen, and of having a jufter notion of people's fentiments of him, than a youth of very high rank at a much more advanced age; for it is very difficult for any perfon to find out that he is defpifed while he continues to be flattered.

So far, therefore, from being furprifed that diffipation, weaknefs, and ignorance, are fo prevalent among thofe who are born to great fortunes and high rank, we ought to be aftonifhed to fee fo great a number of men of virtue, diligence, and genius, among them as there is. And if the number be proportionably greater in England than in

any

any other country, which I believe is the cafe, this muft proceed from the impartial difcipline of our public fchools, and the equitable treatment which boys of the greateft rank receive from their comrades. Sometimes the natural, manly fentiments they acquire from their fchool companions, ferve as an antidote againft the childifh, fophiftical notions with which weak or defigning men endeavour to infpire them in after-life.

The nature of the Britifh conftitution contributes alfo to form a greater number of men of talents among the wealthy and the great, than are to be found in other countries ; becaufe it opens a wider field for ambition than any other government ;—and ambition excites thofe exertions which produce talents.

But, continued I, you muft acknowledge that it would be improper to form a judgment of the Englifh genius, by famples taken from men who have greater temptations

tions to indolence, and fewer fpurs to application than others.

My difputant ftill contefted the point, and
afferted, that high birth gave a native dignity and elevation to the mind ;—that dif-
tinctions and honours were originally introduced into families by eminent abilities
and great virtues ;—that when a man of illuftrious birth came into a company, or
even when his name was mentioned, this
naturally raifed a recollection of the great
actions and fhining qualities of the eminent
perfon who had firft acquired thofe honours ;—that a confcioufnefs of this muft
naturally ftimulate the prefent poffeffor to
imitate the virtues of his anceftors ;—that
his degenerating would fubject him to the
higheft degree of cenfure, as the world
could not, without indignation, behold indolence and vice adorned with the rewards
of activity and virtue.

I might have difputed this affertion, that
honours and titles are always the rewards of

virtue; and could have produced abund-
dance of inftances of the oppofite propofi-
tion. But I allowed that they often were fo,
and that hereditary honours in a family always ought to have, and fometimes had,
the effect which he fuppofed: but thefe
conceffions being made in their fulleft extent, ftill he would do injuftice to the Englifh, by forming a judgment of their national character, from what he had obferved
of the temper, manners, and genius of
thofe Englifhmen with whom he had been
acquainted in foreign countries; becaufe
three-fourths of them were, in all probability, men of fortune, without having family or high birth to boaft of; fo that they
had the greateft inducements to indolence,
without poffeffing the motives to virtuous
exertions, which influence people of high
rank.—For, though it rarely happened in
other countries, it was very common in
England for men of all the various profeffions and trades to accumulate very great
fortunes,

fortunes, which, at their death, falling to their fons, thefe young men, without hav- ing had a fuitable education, immediately fet up for gentlemen, and run over Europe in the characters of Milords Anglois, game, purchafe pictures, mutilated ftatues, and miftreffes, to the aftonifhment of all behold- ers: And, confcious of the blot in their efcutcheon, they think it is incumbent on them to wafh it out, and make up for the impurity of their blood, by plunging deeper into the ocean of extravagance than is ne- ceffary for a man of hereditary fafhion.

Here our converfation ended, and the gentleman promifed that he would abide by the idea he had formed of the Englifh na- tion, from the works of Milton, Locke, and Newton, and the characters of Raleigh, Hambden, and Sidney.

LETTER LI.

Frankfort.

AMONG the remarkable things in Frankfort the inns may be reckoned. Two in particular, the Emperor and the Red Houfe, for cleanlinefs, conveniency, and number of apartments, are fuperior to any I ever faw on the continent, and vie with our moft magnificent inns in England.

At thefe, as at all other inns in Germany and Switzerland, there is an ordinary, at which the ftrangers may dine and fup. This is called the Table d'Hôte, from the circumftance of the landlord's fitting at the bottom of the table, and carving the victuals. The fame name for an ordinary is ftill retained in France, tho' the landlord does not

fit

fit at the table, which was the cafe formerly in that country, and ftill is the cuftom
in Germany.

There are no private lodgings to be had
here, as in London, nor any hôtels garnis as
in Paris.   Strangers therefore retain apartments at the inn during the whole time of
their refidence in any of the towns.   And
travellers of every denomination in this
country, under the rank of fovereign princes, make no fcruple of eating occafionally
at the Table d'Hôte of the inn where they
lodge, which cuftom is univerfally followed
by ftrangers from every country on the
continent of Europe.

Many of our countrymen, however, who
defpife œconomy, and hate the company of
ftrangers, prefer eating in their own apartments to the Table d'Hôte, or any private
table to which they may be invited.

It would be arrogance in any body to difpute the right which every free-born Eng-

Vol. II.   C   lifhman

lifhman has to follow his own inclination
in this particular: Yet when people wifh to
avoid the company of ftrangers, it ftrikes
me, that they might indulge their fancy as
completely at home as abroad; and while
they continue in that humour, I cannot
help thinking that they might fave themfelves the inconveniency and expence of
travelling.

The manners and genius of nations, it is
true, are not to be learnt at inns; nor is
the moft felect company to be found at public ordinaries; yet a perfon of obfervation,
and who is fond of the ftudy of character,
will fometimes find inftruction and entertainment at both. He there fees the inhabitants of the country on a lefs ceremonious
footing than he can elfewhere, and hears
the remarks of travellers of every degree.

The firft care of a traveller certainly
fhould be, to form an acquaintance and fome
degree of intimacy with the principal people

ple in every place where he intends to refide ;—to accept invitations to their family
parties, and attend their focieties;—to entertain them at his apartments, when that
can be conveniently done, and endeavour to
acquire a juft notion of their government,
cuftoms, fentiments, and manner of living.
—Thofe who are fond of the ftudy of man,
which, with all due deference to the philofophers who prefer that of beafts, birds,
and butterflies, is not unnatural philofophy,
will mix occafionally with all degrees of
people, and, when not otherwife engaged,
will not fcruple to take a feat at the Table
d'Hôte.

It is faid that low people are fometimes
to be found at thefe ordinaries. This to be
fure is a weighty objection; but then it
fhould be remembered, that it is within the
bounds of poffibility that men, even engaged
in commerce, may have liberal minds; and
may be able to give as diftinct accounts of
what is worthy of obfervation, as if they

had

had been as idle as people of the higheſt faſhion through the whole of their lives. A man muſt have a very turgid idea of his own grandeur, if he cannot ſubmit, in a foreign country, to dine at table with a perſon of inferiour rank; eſpecially as he will meet, at the ſame time, with others of equal, or ſuperior rank to himſelf: For all etiquette of this nature is waved even in Germany at the Tables d'Hôtes.

A knowledge of the charaĉters of men, as they appear varied in different ſituations and countries —the ſtudy of human nature indeed in all its forms and modifications, is highly intereſting to the mind, and worthy the attention of the greateſt man. This is not to be perfeĉtly attained in courts and palaces. The inveſtigator of nature muſt viſit her in humbler life, and put himſelf on a level with the men whom he wiſhes to know.

It

It is generally found, that thofe who poffefs real greatnefs of mind, never hefitate
to overleap the obftacles, and defpife the
forms, which may ftand in the way of their
acquiring this ufeful knowledge.

The moft powerful of all arguments
againft entirely declining to appear at the
public table of the inn, is, that in this
country it is cuftomary for the ladies themfelves, when on a journey, to eat there; and
my partiality for the Table d'Hôte may
poffibly be owing in fome degree to my
having met, at one of them, with two of
the handfomeft women that I have feen
fince I have been in this country, which
abounds in female beauty.

There is more expreffion in the countenances of French women; but the ladies in
Germany have the advantage in the fairnefs
of their fkin, and the bloom of their complexion.   They have a greater refemblance
to Englifh women than to French; yet they

differ

differ confiderably from them both.—I do not know how to give an idea of the various fhades of expreffion, which, if, I miftake not, I can diftinguifh in the features of the fex in thefe three countries.

A handfome French woman, befides the eafe of her manner, has commonly a look of cheerfulnefs and great vivacity.— She appears willing to be acquainted with you, and feems to expect that you fhould addrefs her.

The manner of an Englifh woman is not fo devoid of reftraint; and a ftranger, efpecially if he be a foreigner, may obferve a look which borders on difdain in her countenance. Even among the lovelieft features, fomething of a fulky air often appears. While their beauty allures, this in fome degree checks that freedom of addrefs which you might ufe to the Frenchwoman, and interefts your vanity more, by

giving

giving the idea of the difficulties you have
to conquer.

A German beauty, without the ſmart
air of the one, or the reſerve of the other,
has generally a more placid look than
either.

C 4

LETTER LII.

Frankfort.

SEVERAL individuals here are fond of diſtinguiſhing themſelves by their paſ-ſion for the fine arts, and ſtrangers are in-formed, that it is well worth while to viſit certain private collections of paintings which are to be ſeen at Frankfort.

You know I am no connoiſſeur; and if I were, ſhould not take up your time in deſcribing them, or giving a criticiſm on their ſubject. For though I have ſeen them, you have not; and nothing, in my opinion, can be more unintelligible and tireſome to the Reader, than criticiſms on paintings which he has not ſeen. I ſhall only ob-ſerve, that as all theſe collections have ac-quired the eſteem and approbation of the

proprietors,

proprietors, which I prefume was the chief
end of their creation, they are certainly in-
titled to refpect from every unconcerned
fpectator.———One of them in particular
muft be very valuable, on account of the
prodigious fum of money which the prefent poffeffor was offered for it, and which
he refufed as inadquate to its worth;
though the fum offered would have at once
made the gentleman eafy in his circumftances, which I am forry to fay, is far
from being the cafe.   This anecdote cannot be doubted, for I had it from his own
mouth.

It is ftill more the fafhion here to form
cabinets of natural curiofities.   Befides the
repofitories of this kind, which are to be
feen at the courts of the princes, many individuals all over Germany have Mufeums
in their houfes, and ftrangers cannot pay
their court better, than by requefting permiffion to fee them.   This would be an
eafy piece of politenefs, if the ftranger were
                    ·   allowed

allowed to take a view, and walk away
when he thought proper. But the mif-
fortune is, that the proprietor attends on
thefe occafions, and gives the hiftory of
every piece of ore, petrifaction, foffil-wood,
and monfter that is in the collection. And
as this lecture is given gratis, he affumes
the right of making it as long as he pleafes:
fo that requefting a fight of a private collection of natural curiofities, is a more
ferious matter than people are aware of.

The Duke of Hamilton has brought himfelf into a fcrape, out of which I imagine
it will be difficult to extricate him. Being
unacquainted with the trouble which thefe
gentlemen give themfelves on fuch occafions, he has expreffed an inclination to
three or four virtuofi to fee their cabinets.
I attended him on his firft vifitation yefterday. The gentleman made an unufual
exertion to pleafe his Grace. He faid, being fully convinced of his tafte for natural
philofophy, in which people of his high
rank

rank were never deficient, he would therefore take pleasure to explain every particular in the collection with the greatest deli-
beration.   He had kept himself disengaged
the whole forenoon on purpose, and had
given orders not to be interrupted.   He
then descanted on each particular in the
collection, with such minuteness and perfeverance, as completely satiated His Grace's
curiosity, and gave him such a knowledge
of earths, crystals, agates, pyrites, mar-
casites, petrifactions, metals, semi-metals,
&c. &c. as will, I dare swear, serve him
for the rest of his life.

Caffel.

I began this letter at Frankfort, not fuf-
pecting that our departure would be so sud-
den.   But as the day approached on which
we had been promised the fight of another
cabinet of curiosities, I found the Duke's
impatience to be gone increase every moment.

ment. So fending our apology to the proprietors of two or three which he had afked permiffion to vifit, we paffed one day with Madame de Barkhaufe's family, and another with Mr. Gogle's, and then bidding a hafty adieu to our other acquaintances at Frankfort, we fet out for this place. We flept the firft night at Marburg, and on the fecond, about midnight, arrived at Caffel.

As the ground is quite covered with fnow, the roads bad, and the pofts long, we were obliged to take fix horfes for each chaife, which, after all, in fome places moved no fafter than a couple of hearfes. The Duke bore this with wonderful ferenity, contemplating the happy evafion he had made from the cabinets at Frankfort. A flave who had efcaped from the mines could not have fhown greater fatisfaction. His good humour remained proof againft all the phlegm and obftinacy of the German poftillions, of which one who has not travelled

in

in the extremity of the winter, and when the roads are covered with fnow, through this country, can form no idea.

The contraft of charaƈter between the French and Germans is ftrongly illuftrated in the behaviour of the poftillions of the two countries.

A French poftillion is generally either laughing, or fretting, or finging, or fwearing, all the time he is on the road. If a hill or a bad road oblige him to go flow, he will of a fudden fall a cracking his whip above his head for a quarter of an hour together, without rhyme or reafon; for he knows the horfes cannot go a bit fafter, and he does not intend they fhould. All this noife and emotion, therefore, means nothing; and proceeds entirely from that abhorrence of quiet which every Frenchman fucks in with his mother's milk.

A German poftillion, on the contrary, drives four horfes with all poffible tranquillity.

lity. He neither fings, nor frets, nor laughs: he only fmokes;—and when he comes near a narrow defile, he founds his trumpet to prevent any carriage from entering at the other end till he has got through. If you call to him to go fafter, he turns about, looks you in the face, takes his pipe from his mouth, and fays, Yaw, Mynheer, —yaw, yaw; and then proceeds exactly in the fame pace as before. He is no way affected whether the road be good or bad; whether it rains, or fhines, or fnows:— And he feems to be totally regardlefs of the people whom he drives, and equally callous to their reproach or applaufe. He has one object of which he never lofes fight, which is, to conduct your chaife and the contents from one poft to another, in the manner he thinks beft for himfelf and the horfes. And unlefs his pipe goes out (in which cafe he ftrikes his flint and rekindles it), he feems not to have another idea during the whole journey.

†   Your

Your beſt courſe is to let him take his
own way at firſt, for it will come to that at
laſt.—All your noiſe and bluſter are vain.

Non vultus inſtantis tyranni

Mente quatit ſolida, neque Auſter

Dux inquieti turbidus Adriæ

Nec fulminantis magna Jovis manus*.

* Not the proud tyrant's fierceſt threat,
　　Nor ſtorms that from their dark retreat
　　　The lawleſs ſurges wake ;
　　Not Jove's dread bolt that ſhakes the pole,
　　The firmer purpoſe of his ſoul,
　　　With all its power can ſhake.
BLACKLOCKE.

LETTER LIII.

THE attention and civilities which are paid to the Duke of Hamilton by this court, have induced us to remain longer than we intended at our arrival.

As you feem curious to know how we pafs our time, and the ftyle of living here, I fhall give you a fketch of one day, which, with little variation, may give you an idea of all the reft.

We generally employ the morning and forenoon in ftudy. We go to the palace about half an hour before dinner is ferved, where we find all the officers, who have been invited, affembled in a large room. The Landgrave foon appears, and continues converfing with the company till his

confort

confort arrives with the princefs Charlotte, and fuch ladies as they have thought proper to invite.

The company then walk to the dining parlour, where there are about thirty covers every day, and the fame number in a room adjoining. The doors being left open between thefe apartments, the whole forms in a manner but one company. The ftrangers, and fuch officers as are not under the rank of colonel, dine at their Highneffes table.

The repaft continues about two hours, during which the converfation is carried on with fome little appearance of conftraint, and rather in a low voice, except when either of their highneffes fpeaks to any perfon feated at a little diftance.

After dinner the company returns to the room where they firft affembled. In this they remain till the Landgrave retires, which he ufually does within about a quar-

Vol. II.   D   ter

ter of an hour. Soon after, the company separates till seven in the evening, when they again affemble.

The Landgrave plays conftantly at Cavaniolle, a kind of lottery, where no addrefs or attention is requifite, and which needs hardly interrupt converfation. It requires about a dozen players to make his party.

The Landgravine plays at Quadrille, and choofes her own party every night.—Other card-tables are fet in the adjoining rooms, for the conveniency of any who choofe to play. The gaming continues about a couple of hours. The Landgrave then falutes her Highnefs on both cheeks, and retires to his own apartments, while fhe and the reft of the company go to fupper. At this repaft there is lefs formality, and of confequence more eafe and gaiety, than at dinner.

When

When her Highnefs rifes from table, moft part of the company attend her up ftairs to a fpacious anti-chamber, where fhe remains converfing a few minutes, and then retires.

Thefe general forms are fometimes varied by a concert in the Landgrave's apartments. There are alfo certain days of Gala, which are only diftinguifhed by the company's being more numerous, and better dreffed, than ufual: two circumftances which do not add a vaft deal to the pleafure of the entertainment.

During the Carnival, there were two or three mafquerades. On thefe occafions the court affemble about fix in the evening, the men being all in Dominos, and the ladies in their ufual drefs, or with the addition of a few fanciful ornaments, according to the particular tafte of each.

They amufe themfelves with cards and converfation till the hour of fupper. Dur-

ing

ing this interval, a gentleman of the court carries a parcel of tickets in his hat, equal to the number of men in company. Thefe are prefented to the ladies, each of whom draws one. Tickets in the fame manner are prefented to the men, who take one a-piece, which they keep till the card-playing is finifhed.

The officer then calls number One, up-on which the couple who are poffeffed of that number come forward, and the gentleman leads the lady into the fupper-room, fits by her, and is her partner for the reft of the evening. In the fame manner every other number is called.

After fupper, all' the company put on their mafks. Her Highnefs is led into the mafquerade room. The reft follow, each lady being handed by her partner. The Landgravine and her partner walk to the upper end of the room.—The next couple ftop at a fmall diftance below them;

them; the third next to the second, and
so on till this double file reaches from the
top to the bottom of the hall. If there
are any supernumeraries, they must retire
to the sides.—From this arrangement you
expect a country dance:—a minuet however is intended:—the music begins, and
all the maskers on the floor, consisting of
twenty or thirty couple, walk a minuet
together. This, which is rather a con-
fused affair, being over, every body sits
down, the Landgravine excepted, who
generally dances nine or ten minuets suc-
cessively with as many different gentlemen.
She then takes her seat till the rest of the
company have danced minuets, which being
over, the cotillons and country-dances begin, and continue till four or five in the
morning.

Her Highness is a very beautiful woman,
graceful in her person, and of a gay and
sprightly character. She is in danger of

D 3   growing

growing corpulent, an inconveniency not uncommon in Germany, but which she endeavours to retard by ufing a great deal of exercife.

Befides the company who fup at court, the rooms were generally crowded with mafks from the town, fome of whom are in fancy-dreffes, and keep themfelves concealed all the time. And although thofe who came from the court are known when, they enter the mafquerade rooms, many of them flip out afterwards, change their drefs, and return to amufe themfelves, by teafing their friends in their affumed characters, as is ufual at mafquerades.

The country dances are compofed of all perfons promifcuoufly, who incline to join in them.—Two women of pleafure, who had come to pafs the Carnival at Caffel in the exercife of their profeffion, and were well known to many of the officers, danced

every

every mafquerade night in the country-
dance, which her Highnefs led down ; for
the mafk annihilates ceremony, puts every
body on a footing, and not unfrequently,
while it conceals the face moft effectually,
ferves fo much the more to difcover the real
character and inclinations of the wearer.

D 4

LETTER LIV.

NEXT to the Electors of the Empire, the Landgrave of Heffe Caffel is one of the greateft Princes in Germany ; and even of thofe, the electors of Bohemia, Bavaria, Saxony, and Hanover, only are richer and more powerful than he. His country is in general hilly, with a great deal of wood, but interfperfed with fertile vallies and corn-fields. The large fubfidies this court received from Britain during the two laft wars, with what is given in the time of peace, by way of retaining fee, have greatly contributed to the prefent flourifh-ing ftate of its financcs.

The reigning Prince forfook the Pro-teftant faith about twenty years ago, and made

made a public profeffion of the Roman Catholic religion, in the life-time of the late Landgrave, his father. This gave great uneafinefs to the old Prince, and alarmed his fubjects, who are all Proteftants.

The ftates of the Landgraviate were affembled on this important occafion, and fuch meafures taken as were judged neceffary to maintain the religion and conftitution of the country againft any future attempt to fubvert them. The Hereditary Prince was excluded from all fhare in the education of his fons, who were put under the tuition of the Princefs Mary of Great Britain, his firft wife, living at that time feparate from her hufband. The eldeft fon, upon his father's acceffion to the Landgraviate, was put in poffeffion of the county of Hanau; fo that the inhabitants have felt no inconveniency from the change of their Prince's religion. And as he himfelf has reaped no earthly advantage,

either

either in point of honour or profit, by his converfion, it is prefumable, that his Highnefs's hopes are now limited to the rewards which may await him in another world.

This Prince keeps on foot 16,000 men in time of peace, difciplined according to the Pruffian plan, the Landgrave himfelf having the rank of Field Marfhal in the Pruffian army. The Prince is fond of exercifing them; but not having a houfe on purpofe, as the Prince of Heffe Darmftadt has, he takes that amufement when the weather is very bad in the diningroom of his palace, where I have frequently feen two or three hundred of the firft battalion of guards perform their manœuvres with all poffible dexterity.

The Prince of Saxe-Gotha, brother to the late Princefs of Wales, has a regiment in the Landgrave's fervice, and refides at Caffel.

The

The perſon who has the chief management in military affairs, is General Scli-
ven, a man of an exceeding juſt and accurate underſtanding, which he has finely
cultivated by reading and reflection.

I have the happineſs to be intimately
acquainted with many other officers in this
ſervice.—An open manner, and undeſign-
ing civility, diſtinguiſh the German character; qualities which naturally baniſh reſerve, and inſpire confidence. And what
makes the converſation of theſe gentlemen
ſtill more agreeable and intereſting to me,
is the juſtice they ſeem fond of rendering
to the bravery of the Britiſh troops with
whom they ſerved. They always mention
the names of Granby, Waldgrave, and
Kingſley, with the higheſt encomiums,
and ſpeak with affectionate regard of ſome
officers with whom they were more intimately acquainted, particularly Mr. Keith,
now at Vienna, and Colonel John Max-
well, whom they applaud as one of the
braveſt

braveft and moft active officers that ferved in the allied army; and feem fond of mentioning inftances of the amazing intrepidity of the Britifh grenadiers whom he commanded.

Befides thofe actually in the Landgrave's fervice, there are fome other perfons of note who refide at Caffel. I fometimes pafs an afternoon with old General Zaftrow, who had the command of the garrifon of Schweidnitz, when it was furprifed by the Auftrian general Laudohn.

If you recollect, that important place had been taken from the Pruffians in the year 1757, by Count Nadafti. It was blockaded by the King of Pruffia in the winter of that fame year, and furrendered to him in fpring 1758, after one half of the garrifon had fallen in defending the place. In the year 1761, Laudohn retook it almoft in fight of the Pruffian monarch, by the moft brilliant coup-de-main that perhaps ever was ftruck.

The

The King's army and Laudohn's were both in the neighbourhood of Schweidnitz. The latter could not attempt a regular fiege, while he was watched by fuch an enterprifing enemy. But obferving that the King had moved at a greater diftance than ufual from the town, and knowing that more than one half of the garrifon had been drafted, he refolved on an enterprife as bold as it was fagacious. One morning early this vigilant commander, taking the advantage of a thick fog, marched his army to the town of Schweidnitz in four divifions. Scaling ladders were applied to the ramparts, and fome of the Auftrians had actually entered the town, before they were obferved by the centinels.

The garrifon being at laft roufed, attacked the affailants in a furious manner.— The confufion was increafed by the blowing up of a powder magazine, which deftroyed great numbers on both fides. The Governor was taken prifoner, fighting fword in hand

hand on the ramparts, and the town furrendered.

This exploit eſtabliſhed the reputation of
Laudohn, while poor Zaſtrow, according
to the uſual fate of the unfortunate, became a prey to the calumny of the unfeel-
ing and ungenerous. He demanded a trial
by a court martial.—The King ſaid there
was no occaſion for that, as he did not ac-
cuſe him of any crime.—But he did not
judge it expedient to employ him in any
command after this misfortune.

I have heard the old man relate all the
particulars of that affair, and the account
he gave has been confirmed to me by officers well informed, and unconnected with
him.

A company of French comedians are
lately arrived here, which forms a new
reſource for the court. They remain ſix
weeks, or two months. The Landgrave
pays them a ſtipulated ſum for acting twice

‡   a week

a week during that time; and they have fcarcely any emolument befide; for the inhabitants of Caffel, who are Calvinifts, fhew no great paffion for dramatic entertainments.

The playhoufe is neat, though fmall. The front gallery, with a convenient room behind, is appropriated to the court. When the Prince or Princefs ftands up, whether between the acts, or in the time of the reprefentation, all the audience, pit, box, and gallery, immediately arife, and remain in a ftanding pofture till their fovereign fit down.

Since the arrival of thefe players, the court has been uncommonly brilliant, and the Gala days more frequent. Yefterday was a very fplendid one. I then obferved in the drawing-room two perfons, neither of whom is a Heffian, faluting each other with great politenefs and apparent regard. A little after, one of them touched my fhoulder, and, pointing to the other, whifpered

whifpered in my ear,—Prenez garde, Monfieur, de cet homme; c'eft un grand co-
quin.

The other within a few minutes came
to me, faying, Croyez vous, Monfieur, que
vouz puiffiez reconnoitre un fou fi je vous
le montrois ?—Le voilà, added he, fhowing
the perfon who had whifpered me before.

I have been fince told, by thofe who
know both, that each had hit exactly upon
the other's character.

This little trait I have mentioned merely
on account of its fingularity, and to fhow
you how very different the manners of this
court, and the fentiments of the courtiers
here with regard to each other, are from
thofe at St. James's.

LETTER LV.

Caſſel.

THE city of Caſſel is ſituated on the river Fulda. It conſiſts of an old and new town. The former is the largeſt and moſt irregular. The new town is well built; and there, as you may believe, the nobility and officers of the court have their houſes. The ſtreets are beautiful, but not over-crowded with inhabitants.

Beſides the large chateau in the town of Caſſel, which is the Landgrave's winter reſidence, he has ſeveral villas and caſtles in different parts of his dominions. Immediately without the town, there is a very beautiful building, in which he dwells for the moſt part of the ſummer. The apart-

VOL. II.   E   ments

ments there are neat and commodious, some
of them adorned with antique statues of
considerable value.

None of the rooms are spacious enough
to admit of exercising any considerable
number of the troops within their walls;
but his Highness sometimes indulges in
this favourite recreation on the top of this
villa, which has a flat roof, most convenient
for that purpose.

Around this are some noble parks and
gardens, with a very complete orangery.
There is also a menagerie, with a considerable collection of curious animals. I
saw there a very fine lioness, which has
lately lost her husband—an elephant—three
camels in fine condition, one of them milk-
white, the other two grey, and much
taller than the elephant;—an African deer,
a fierce and lively animal, with a skin beau-
tifully spotted;—a very tall rain-deer—several leopards—a bear, and a great variety
of monkies. The collection of birds is
                                          still

ftill more complete, a great many of which are from the Eaft Indies.

In the academy of arts, which is fituated in the new town, are fome valuable antiques, and other curiofities, among which is a St. John in Mofaic, done after a picture of Raphaël's, with the following infcription below it:

IMAGINEM S. JOHANNES
EX ITALIA ADVENAM
IN RARUM RARÆ INDUSTRIÆ HUMANÆ MONUMENTUM
HANC COLLOCARI JUSSIT
FREDERICUS II. HASSIÆ LANDGR.
A. M.D.CCLXV.

But this art of copying paintings in Mofaic work, I underftand has of late been brought to a much greater degree of perfection at Rome.

In the veftibule is placed the trunk of a laurel tree, with this infcription on the wall behind it:

QUÆ
PER OCTO PRINCIPUM CATTORUM ÆTATIS
IN AMÆNIS INCLYTI; CASSEL.
VIRIDARII SPATIAM FLORUIT
LAURUS
ALT. CIRCITER LIV. LAT. IV. PED. RHENAN.
AD TEMPORA HEROUM
SERENISS. DOMUS HASSIÆ
CORONIS CINGENDA,
SENIO, SED NON IMPLORIS, EMORTUA EST
NE VERO TOTA PERIRET
ARBOR APOLLINI SACRA
TRUNCUM IN MUSEO SERVARI JUSSIT
FREDERICUS II. H. L.
A. M.D.CCLXIII.

They also show a sword, which was consecrated by the Pope, and sent to one of the Princes of this family at his setting out on an expedition to, the Holy Land. What havoc this sacred weapon made among the infidels I cannot say.—It has a very venerable appearance for a sword, and yet seems little the worse for wear.

Near the old chateau, and a little to one side, is a colonnade of small pillars lately built, and intended as an ornament to the

*   ancient

ancient caftle, though in a very different ftyle of architecture. The flimnefs of their form appears the more remarkable on account of their vicinity to this Gothic ftructure.

Some time fince, a mountebank came to Caffel, who, befides many other wonderful feats, pretended that he could fwallow and digeft ftones. A Heffian officer walking before the chateau with an Englifh gentleman, who then happened to be at Caffel, afked him, What he thought of the fine new colonnade ?—It is very fine indeed, replied the ftranger ; but if you wifh it to be durable, you ought to take care not to allow the mountebank to walk this way before breakfaft.

.. Nothing in the country of Heffe is more worthy the admiration of travellers, than the Gothic temple and cafcade at Wafen-ftein. There was originally at this place an old building, which was ufed by the Princes of this family as a kind of hunting-

E 3   houfe.

houſe. It is ſituated near the bottom of a high mountain, and has been enlarged and improved at different times. But the preſent Landgrave's grandfather, who was a Prince of equal taſte and magnificence, formed, upon the face of the mountain oppoſite to this houſe, a ſeries of artificial cataracts, caſcades, and various kinds of water-works, in the nobleſt ſtyle that can be imagined.

The principal caſcades are in the middle, and on each ſide are ſtairs of large black ſtones of a flinty texture, brought from a rock at a conſiderable diſtance. Each of theſe ſtairs conſiſts of eight hundred ſteps, leading from the bottom to the ſummit of the mountain; and when the works are allowed to play, the water flowing over them forms two continued chains of ſmaller caſcades. At convenient diſtances, as you aſcend, are four platforms, with a ſpacious baſon in each; alſo grottos and caves ornamented with ſhell-work ſtatues

of

of Naïads, and sea divinities.—One grotto, in particular, called the Grotto of Neptune and Amphitrite, is happily imagined, and well executed.

The water rushes from the summit of this mountain in various shapes:—Sometimes in detached cascades, sometimes in large sheets like broad crystalline mirrors; at one place, it is broken by a rock consisting of huge stones, artificially placed for that purpose.—There are also fountains which eject the water in columns of five or six inches diameter to a considerable height.

All this must have a very brilliant effect when viewed from the bottom. This sight, however, I did not enjoy: for there has been a continued frost ever since we have been at Cassel; and when I visited Wasenstein, the fields were covered with snow, which did not prevent my going to the top, though it made the ascent by the stairs exceedingly difficult.

E 4

On

On the higheſt part of the mountain, a Gothic temple is built, and upon the top of that an obeliſk, which is crowned by a coloſſal ſtatue of Hercules leaning on his club, in the attitude of the Farneſe Hercules. This figure is of copper, and thirty feet in height. There is a ſtaircaſe within the club by which a man may aſcend, and have a view of the country from a window at the top.

Waſenſtein, upon the whole, is infinitely the nobleſt work of the kind I ever ſaw, I have been aſſured, there is nothing equal to it in Europe. It has not the air of a modern work, but rather conveys the idea of Roman magnificence.

We think of leaving this within a few days for Brunſwick.—I ſhall not cloſe my letter till we get to Gottingen, where we may probably ſtay a ſhort time.

P. S. The Duke and I took our leave of the Court and our friends yeſterday, and

actually

actually fet out from Caffel this morning; but finding the roads entirely overflowed by the extraordinary fwelling of the Fulda, we were obliged to return. A great thaw for fome days paft diffolving the fnow and ice, has occafioned this fwelling, and rendered the roads impaffable.

After taking leave we could not appear again at court, but dined at one of the meffes with the officers.—From this party I am juft returned, and finding it uncertain when we may get to Gottingen, I fend this to-night.

Adieu,

LETTER LVI.

Brunfwick.

AS foon as the roads were paffable, we left Caffel, and arrived, not without difficulty and fome rifk, at Munden, a town fituated in a vale, where the Fulda, being joined by another river, takes the name of the Wefer.

This town feems to run fome danger from inundations. The road, for a confiderable way before we entered it, and the ftreets neareft the river, were ftill overflowed when we paffed.

We went on the fame night to Gottingen, an exceedingly neat and well-built town, fituated in a beautiful country. The Univerfity founded here by George the Second has a confiderable reputation. We

made

made but a short stay at Gottingen, and arrived about a month since at Brunswick.

The Duke of Hamilton had been expected here for some time, and was received by this court with every mark of attention and regard. He was pressed to accept of apartments within the palace, which he ' thought proper to decline. We sleep every night at private lodgings; but may be said to live at court, as we constantly dine, pass the evening, and sup there, except two days in every week that we dine with the Hereditary Prince and Princess at their apartments.

The family of Brunswick Wolfenbuttle derives not greater lustre from its antiquity, from having given empresses to Germany, and from having a younger branch on the throne of Britain, than from some living characters now belonging to it.

The reigning Duke has that style of conversation, those manners and disposi-

I   tions,

tions, which, in an inferior ftation of life, would acquire him the character of a fenfible, worthy gentleman.

The Duchefs is the favourite fifter of the King of Pruffia. She is fond of ftudy, and particularly addicted to metaphyfical inquiries, which, happily, have not fhaken, but confirmed her belief in Chriftianity.

The military fame and public character of Duke Ferdinand are known to all Europe.—In private life, he is of a ceremonious politenefs, fplendid in his manner of living, attentive even to the minutiæ of his toilet, and fond of variety and magnificence in drefs.

He has lived conftantly at his brother's court fince the Duke of Hamilton came to Brunfwick; but he generally paffes the fummer in the country.

The Hereditary Prince ferved under his uncle during the laft war, and commanded detached parties of the army with various fuccefs.

fuccefs. His activity, courage, and thirft
of glory, were always confpicuous; but
his youthful ardour has been fince mel-
lowed by time, ftudy, and reflection; and
if he fhould again appear in the field as
a general, it is imagined that he will be as
much diftinguifhed for prudence, policy,
and judgment, as he ever was for fpirit and
enterprize. He has at prefent the rank of
Lieutenant General in the King of Pruffia's
fervice, and the command of the garrifon
at Halberftadt.

I fay nothing of his Princefs:—Her
open cheerful character is well known in
England, and her affection for her native
country is in no degree diminifhed by abfence.

The Prince Leopold is a very amiable
young man. He feems much attached to
the Duke of Hamilton, with whom he lives
on an intimate and friendly footing.

His

His fifter, the Princefs Augufta, is greatly beloved by every body, on account of her obliging temper and excellent difpofition.

Thefe illuftrious perfons always dine and fup together, except two days in the week, as I have already faid. With them the officers of the court, and the ftrangers who are invited, make a company of about twenty or thirty at table.

In the evening the affembly is more numerous. There is a large table for Vingt-un, the Duchefs preferring this game, becaufe a great number of people may be engaged in it together. The reigning Duke and Prince Ferdinand always join in this game.

The Hereditary Princefs forms a Quadrille party for herfelf: Her hufband never plays at all. The whole is intended merely for paftime, all kinds of gaming being difcouraged. The Duchefs in particular always puts a very moderate ftake on her cards.

cards.—A man muſt have very bad luck to loſe above twenty piſtoles in an evening; ſo we are in no danger from gaming while at this court.

One wing of the palace is occupied by the Hereditary Prince's family. He has at preſent three ſons and as many daughters, all of the fair complexion, which diſtinguiſhes every branch of the Brunſwick line.

A few days ago, I accompanied Prince Leopold and the Duke of Hamilton on a viſit to Duke Ferdinand, who was then at his houſe in the country, about ſix miles from this place. In that retreat he paſſes the greateſt part of his time. He is fond of gardening, and is now employed in laying out and dreſſing the ground, in what is called the Engliſh taſte.

His Serene Highneſs conducted the Duke round all his park, and ſhewed him his plans and improvements. The greateſt obſtacle to the completely beautifying this place,

place, arifes from the furface of the country being a dead flat, and incapable of great
variety.

The houfe is furrounded by a Foffé,
and contains a great number of apartments.
The walls of every room are hung with
prints, from the roof to within two feet of
the floor. Perhaps there is not fo complete a collection of framed ones in any
private houfe or palace in the world.
While Prince Ferdinand played at Billiards
with the Duke of Hamilton, I continued
with Prince Leopold examining thefe
prints, and could fcarcely recollect a good
one that I did not find here.

His Highnefs faid it was equally difficult and expenfive to have a collection of
good paintings, and nothing could be
more paltry than a bad one : he had therefore taken the refolution to adorn his houfe
with what he certainly could have good of
its kind ; and, next to fine pictures, he
thought fine prints the moft amufing of all
                                    ornaments.

ornaments. But, added he, with a fmile, every tolerable room is now perfectly covered, and I have lately received a reinforcement of prints from England, which will oblige me to build new apartments to place them in, puifque je fuis toujours accoutumé à donner un pofte honorable aux Anglois.

The company had been invited to breakfaft; but the repaft was a very magnificent dinner, ferved a little earlier than ufual. There were only fix perfons at table; but the number of attendants might without difficulty have ferved a company of thirty. The Prince, who is always in the utmoft degree polite, was on this occafion remarkably affable and gay. He called toafts after the Englifh cuftom, and began himfelf by naming General Conway; he afterwards gave Sir H. Clinton, and continued to toaft fome Britifh officer, as often as it came to his turn.—You may believe it afforded me fatisfaction to have had an opportunity of

VOL. II.   F   obferving

obferving a little of the private life of a perfon who has acted fo confpicuous a part on the theatre of Europe.

As he has not returned to the Pruffian fervice, and feems to enjoy rural amufe-ments, and the converfation of a few friends, it is thought he will not again take a part in public affairs, but for the reft of his life repofe, in this retreat, on the laurels he gathered in fuch abundance during the laft war.

LETTER LVII.

Brunfwick.

THE town of Brunfwick is fituated in a plain, on the banks of the Ocker. The houfes in general are old, but many new buildings have been erected of late, and the city acquires frefh beauty every day.

Fortifications have been the caufe of much calamity to many towns in Germany, having ferved not to defend them, but rather to attract the vengeance of enemies. For this reafon, Caffel, and fome other towns, which wereformerly fortified, are now difmantled. But the fortifications at Brunfwick were of great utility laft war, and on one occafion they faved the town from being pillaged, and afforded Prince

F 2   Frederick,

Frederick, who is now in the Pruffian fervice, an opportunity of performing an action, which, I imagine, gave him more joy than twenty victories. This happened in the year 1761, foon after the battle of Kirch Denkern, when Duke Ferdinand protected Hanover, not by conducting his army into that country, and defending it directly, as the enemy feemed to expect, and probably wifhed; but by diverfion, attacking with ftrong detachments, commanded by the Hereditary Prince, their magazines in Heffe, and thus drawing their attention from Hanover to that quarter.

While the Duke lay encamped at Willhemfthall, watching the motions of Broglio's army, the Marechal being greatly fuperior in numbers, fent a body of 20,000 men, under Prince Xavier of Saxony, who took poffeffion of Wolfenbuttle, and foon after invefted Brunfwick.

Prince Ferdinand, anxious to fave his native city, ventured to detach 5000 of his

army,

army, fmall as it was, under his nephew, Frederick, affifted by General Luckener, with orders to harafs the enemy, and endeavour to raife the fiege. The young Prince, while on his march, fent a foldier with a letter to the Governor, which was wrapped round a bullet, and which the foldier was to fwallow in cafe of his being taken by the enemy.—He had the good fortune to get fafe into the town.—The letter apprifed the commander of the garrifon of the Prince's approach, and particularifed the night and hour when he expected to be at a certain place near the town, requiring him to favour his entrance.

In the middle of the night appointed, the Prince fell fuddenly on the enemy's cavalry, who, unfufpicious of his approach, were encamped carelefly within a mile of the town. They were immediately difperfed, and fpread fuch an alarm among

F 3   the

the infantry, that they alfo retreated with confiderable lofs.

Early in the morning, the young Prince entered Brunfwick, amidft the acclamations of his fellow-citizens, whom he had relieved from the horrors of a fiege.—The Hereditary Prince having deftroyed the French magazines in Heffe, had been recalled by his uncle, and ordered to attempt the relief of Brunfwick. While he was advancing with all poffible fpeed, and had got within a few leagues of the town, he received the news of the fiege being raifed. On his arrival at his father's palace, he found his brother Frederick at table, entertaining the French officers, who had been taken prifoners the preceding night.

The academy of Brunfwick has been new-modelled, and the plan of education improved, by the attention, and under the patronage, of the Hereditary Prince. Students now refort to this academy from many parts of Germany; and there are

generally

generally fome young gentlemen from Britain, who are fent to be educated here.

Such of them as are intended for a military life, will not find fo many advantages united at any other place on the continent, as at the academy of Brunfwick. They will here be under the protection of a family, partial to the Britifh nation;— every branch of fcience is taught by mafters of known abilities;—the young ftudents will fee garrifon duty regularly performed, and may, by the intereft of the Prince, obtain liberty to attend the reviews of the Pruffian troops at Magdeburg and Berlin:—They will have few temptations to expence, in a town where they can fee no examples of extravagance —have few opportunities of diffipation, and none of grofs debauchery.

I paffed a day lately at Wolfenbuttle, which is alfo a fortified city, the ancient refidence of this family.—The public library here is reckoned one of the moft

complete

complete in Germany, and contains many curious manufcripts. They fhowed us fome lettets of Luther, and other original pieces in that reformer's own hand-writing.

Having dined with Colonel Riedefel, who commands a regiment of cavalry in this town, I returned by Saltzdahlen. This is the only palace I ever faw built almoft entirely of wood. There are, neverthelefs, fome very magnificent apartments in it, and a great gallery of pictures, fome of which are allowed by the connoiffeurs to be excellent. I will not invade the province of thefe gentlemen, by prefuming to give my opinion of the merits or defects of the pictures, though I have often heard thofe, who are as ignorant as myfelf, decide upon the interefting fubject of painting, in the moft dogmatic manner. The terms Contour, Attitude, Cafting of Draperies, Charging, Coftumé, Paffion, Manner, Groupe, Out-line, Chiaro Scuro,
Harmony,

Harmony, and Repofe, flowed from their tongues, with a volubility that commanded the admiration of all thofe who could not difcover, that in the liberal ufe of thefe terms confifted all thofe gentlemen's tafte and knowledge of the fine arts.

Confcious of my ignorance in the myfteries of connoiffeurfhip, I fay nothing of the pictures, and prefume only to give my opinion, that the gallery which contains them is a very noble room, being two hundred feet long, fifty broad, and forty high.

In this palace there is alfo a cabinet of china porcelain, containing, as we were told, feven or eight thoufand pieces;—and in another fmaller cabinet, we were fhown a collection of coarfe plates, valuable only on account of their having been painted after defigns of Raphaël.

The

The country about Brunſwick is agreeable. I was particularly pleaſed to ſee ſome gentlemen's ſeats near this town; a ſight very rare in Germany, where, if you avoid towns and courts, you may travel over a great extent of country, without perceiving houſes for any order of men between the Prince and the Peaſant.

I ſpent yeſterday very agreeably, fourteen miles from Brunſwick, at the houſe of Mr. de Weſtphalen. This gentleman attended Duke Ferdinand during the late war in the character of his private ſecretary; an office which he executed entirely to the ſatisfaction of that Prince, whoſe friendſhip and confidence he ſtill retains.

Mr. de Weſtphalen has written the hiſtory of thoſe memorable campaigns, in which his patron had the command of the allied army, and baffled all the efforts of France in Weſtphalia. Though this work has been finiſhed long ſince, the publication

tion has hitherto been delayed for political reafons.   It is to appear, however, at fome future period, and is faid to be a mafterly performance.   Indeed, one would naturally fuppofe this from the remarkable acutenefs and fagacity of the author, who was prefent at the fcenes he defcribes, and knew the fecret intentions of the General, whofe affiftance he has probably had in finifhing the work.

L E T T E R LVIII.

Brunfwick.

WE have had fome mafquerade balls
here of late.—The Court do not go
in proceffion to thefe as at Caffel.—Thofe
who chufe to attend, go feparately when
they find it convenient.

There is a gallery in the mafquerade-
room for the reigning family, where they
fometimes fit without mafks, and amufe
themfelves by looking at the dancers. But
in general they go mafked, and mix in
an eafy and familiar manner with the company.

I am not furprifed that the Germans,
efpecially thofe of high rank, are fond of
mafquerades, being fo much haraffed with
ceremony and form, and cramped by the
diftance

diſtance which birth throws between people who may have a mutual regard for each other. I imagine they are glad to ſeize every opportunity of aſſuming the maſk and domino, that they may taſte the plea-ſures of familiar converſation and ſocial mirth.——In company with the Duke of Hamilton, I once had the honour of dining at the houſe of a general officer. His ſiſter did the honours of the table; and on the Duke's expreſſing his ſurpriſe that he never had ſeen her at court, he was told ſhe could not poſſibly appear there, becauſe ſhe was not noble. This lady, however, was viſited at home by the Sovereign, and every family of diſtinction, all of whom regretted, that the eſtabliſhed cuſtom of their country deprived the court of a perſon whoſe character they valued ſo highly.

The General's rank in the army was a ſufficient paſſport for him, but was of no ſervice to his ſiſter; for this etiquette is
observed

obferved very rigidly with refpect to the natives of Germany, though it is greatly relaxed to ftrangers, particularly the Eng-lifh, who they imagine have lefs regard for birth and title than any other nation.

Public diverfions of every kind are now over for fome time, and the Court is at prefent very thin.—Duke Ferdinand refides in the country. The Hereditary Prince went a few days fince to Haberftadt, where he will remain at leaft a month, to pre-pare the garrifon, and his own regiment in particular, for the grand reviews which are foon to take place. Diligence in duty, and application to the difciplining of the forces, are indifpenfable in this fervice. Without thefe, not all the King's partia-lity to this Prince, or his confanguinity, could fecure to him his uncle's favour for one day, perfonal talents and vigorous ex-ertion being the fole means of acquiring and retaining the favour of this fteady and difcerning monarch.

The

The Hereditary Princefs has left Brunf-wick, and is gone to Zell, and will remain during the abfence of her hufband with her fifter the Queen of Denmark.

The young Prince, Leopold, has also left the Court. He goes directly to Vienna, and it is thought he intends to offer his fervices to the Emperor. If proper encouragement be given, he will go entirely into the Auftrian fervice. In this cafe, he will probably, when a war happens, find himfelf in oppofition to his two brothers; a circumftance not much regarded in Germany, where brothers go into different fervices, with as little hefitation as into different regiments with us.

The ftricteft friendfhip has always fub-fifted between this young man and his fifter, who has been crying almoft without intermiffion fince he went away.

His mother bears this with more compofure, yet her uneafinefs is eafier per-
6   ceived.

ceived. Independent of the abfence of her fon, fhe is diftreffed at the idea of his going into a fervice, where he may be obliged to act in oppofition to her brother *, for whom I find fhe has the greateft affection, as well as the higheft admiration.

* Prince Leopold did not enter into the Auftrian fervice; but after having vifited Vienna, and made the tour of Italy, he returned to Brunfwick.——His uncle, the King of Pruffia, foon after offering him the command of a regiment, he went into the fervice of that monarch, in which he remained till the fpring of the prefent year 1785, when being witnefs to the devaftation occafioned by the overflowing of a river, unmoved by the entreaties of thofe who endeavoured to diffuade him from fo hazardous an enterprize, he embarked in a fmall boat with three watermen, to relieve the inhabitants of a village furrounded by the waters. But before he reached them the boat was drove with volence againft a tree, and overfet; the three boatmen were faved. This amiable Prince alone, being carried down by the impetuofity of the current, perifhed in the fight of thofe he attempted to preferve, difplaying in his death an heoric inftance of that benevolence which had appeared confpicuous through the whole of his life.

That ingenious artift Mr. Northcote, who fo fuccefsfully painted the wonderful efcape of Captain Inglefield, has fince, with equal, if not fuperior energy, finifhed a picture reprefenting the Death of Prince Leopold of Brunfwick.

I was

I was not furprifed to hear her fpeak of him as the greateft man alive; but fhe extends her eulogium to the qualities of his heart, in which fhe is not joined by the opinion of all the world.—She, however, dwells particularly on this, calling him the worthieft of men, the firmeft friend, and the kindeft of brothers :—and as fhe founds her opinion on her own experience alone, fhe has the greateft reafon to think as fhe does; for, by every account, the King has always behaved with high regard and undeviating tendernefs to her.

The departure of Prince Leopold has revived this Princefs's affliction for the untimely fate of two of her fons. One died in the Ruffian camp at the end of the campaign of 1769, in which he had ferved with great diftinction as a volunteer; the other was killed in a fkirmifh towards the end of the laft war; having received a fhot in his throat, he died of the wound fifteen days

VOL. II.   G   after,

after, much regretted by the army, who had formed a high idea of the rifing merit of this gallant youth.

He wrote a letter to his mother in the morning of the day on which he died. In this letter he regrets, that he fhould be ftopped fo foon in the courfe of honour, and laments that he had not been killed in fome memorable action, which would have faved his name from oblivion, or in atchieving fomething worthy of the martial fpirit of his family. He expreffes fatisfaction, however, that his memory would at leaft be dear to fome friends, and that he was certain of living in his mother's affections while fhe fhould exift. He then declares his gratitude to her for all her care and tendernefs, and concludes with thefe expreffions, which I tranflate as near as I can remember—I wifhed the Duchefs to repeat them; but it was with difficulty, and eyes overflowing, that fhe pronounced them once:

once:—" My eyes grow dim—I can fee no
" longer—happy to have employed their
" laft light in exprefling my duty to my
" mother."

G 2

LETTER LIX.

Hanover.

THE Duke of Hamilton having determined to pay his refpects to the Queen of Denmark, before he left this country, chofe to make his vifit while the Hereditary Princefs was with her fifter.

I accompanied him to Zell, and next day waited on the Count and Countefs Dean, to let them know of the Duke's arrival, and to be informed when we could have the honour of being prefented to the Queen.   They both belong to the Princefs of Brunfwick's family, and while I was at breakfaft with them, her Royal Highnefs entered the room, and gave me the information I wanted.

Before

Before dinner, I returned with the Duke to the castle, where we remained till late in the evening. There was a concert of music between dinner and supper, and the Queen seemed in better spirits than could have been expected.

Zell is a small town, without trade or manufactures; the houses are old, and of a mean appearance, yet the high courts of appeal for all the territories of the Electoral House of Brunswick Lunenburg are held here; the inhabitants derive their principal means of subsistence from this circumstance.

This town was severely harassed by the French army at the beginning of the late war, and was afterwards pillaged, in revenge for the supposed infraction of the treaty of Closter-Seven. The Duke de Richlieu had his head-quarters here, when Duke Ferdinand re-assembled the troops who had been disarmed and disperfed, immediately after that convention.

The

The caftle is a ftately building, furrounded by a moat, and ftrongly fortified.
It was formerly the refidence of the Dukes
of Zell, and was repaired lately by order
of the King of Great Britain for the reception of his unfortunate fifter. The apartments are fpacious and convenient, and
now handfomely furnifhed.

The officers of the Court, the Queen's
maids of honour, and other attendants,
have a very genteel appearance, and retain
the moft refpeⅽtful attachment to their ill-
fated miftrefs. The few days we remained
at Zell, were fpent entirely at Court, where
every thing feemed to be arranged in the
ftyle of the other fmall German courts,
and nothing wanting to render the Queen's
fituation as comfortable as circumftances
would admit. But by far her greateft confolation is the company and converfation
of her fifter. Some degree of fatisfaction
appears in her countenance while the Princefs remains at Zell; but the moment fhe

goes

goes away, the Queen, as we were informed, becomes a prey to dejection and
defpondency. The Princefs exerts herfelf
to prevent this, and devotes to her fifter
all the time fhe can fpare from the duties
fhe owes to her own family. Unlike
thofe who take the firft pretext of break-
ing connections which can no longer be
of advantage, this humane Princefs has
difplayed even more attachment to her
fifter fince her misfortunes, than fhe ever
did while the Queen was in the meridian
of her profperity.

The youth, the agreeable countenance,
and obliging manners of the Queen, have
conciliated the minds of every one in this
country. Though fhe was in perfect
health, and appeared cheerful, yet, convinced that her gaiety was affumed, and
the effect of a ftrong effort, I felt an impreffion of melancholy, which it was not
in my power to overcome all the time we
remained at Zell.

G 4

From Zell we went to Hanover, and on the evening of our arrival, had the pleafure of hearing Handel's Meffiah performed. Some of the beft company of this place were affembled on the occafion, and we were here made acquainted with old Field-Marfhal Sporken, and other people of diftinction. Hanover is a neat, thriving, and agreeable city. It has more the air of an Englifh town than any other I have feen in Germany, and the Englifh manners and cuftoms gain ground every day among the inhabitants. The genial influence of freedom has extended from England to this place. Tyranny is not felt, and eafe and fatisfaction appear in the countenances of the citizens.

This town is regularly fortified, and all the works are in exceeding good order. The troops are fober and regular, and perform every effential part of duty well, though the difcipline is not fo rigid as in fome other parts of Germany. Marfhal Sporken,

Sporken, who is the head of the army,
is a man of humanity; and though the
foldiers are feverely punifhed for real
crimes, by the fentence of a court martial,
he does not permit his officers to order
them to be caned for trifles. Caprice is
too apt to blend itfelf with this method of
punifhing, and men of cruel difpofitions
are prone to indulge this diabolical propenfity, under the pretence of zeal for difcipline.

The Hanoverian infantry are not fo tall
as fome of the other German troops, owing
to this, that nobody is forced into the
fervice, the foldiers are all volunteers;
whereas; in other parts of Germany, the
Prince picks the ftouteft and talleft of the
peafants, and obliges them to become foldiers. It is allowed, that in action no
troops can behave better than the Hano-
verians; and it is certain, that defertion
is not fo frequent among them as among
other German troops, which can only be
accounted

accounted for by their not being preſſed into the ſervice, and their being more gently uſed when in it.

It is not the mode here at preſent, to lay ſo much ſtreſs on the tricks of the exerciſe as formerly. The officers in general ſeem to deſpiſe many minutiæ, which are thought of the higheſt importance in ſome other ſervices. It is incredible to what a ridiculous length this matter is puſhed by ſome.

At a certain parade, where the Sovereign himſelf was preſent, and many officers aſſembled, I once ſaw a corpulent general-officer ſtart ſuddenly, as if he had ſeen ſomething preternatural. He immediately waddled towards the ranks with all the expedition of a terrified gander. I could not conceive what had put his Excellency into a commotion ſo little ſuitable to his years and habit of body. While all the ſpectators were a-tiptoe to obſerve the iſſue of this phenomenon, he arrived

at

at the ranks, and in great wrath, which probably had been augmented by the heat acquired in his courſe, he pulled off one of the ſoldier's hats, which it ſeems had not been properly cocked, and adjuſted it to his mind.   Having regulated the military diſcipline in this important particular, he returned to the Prince's right-hand, with a ſtrut expreſſive of the higheſt ſelf-approbation.

Two days after our arrival here, I walked to Hernhauſen, along a magnificent avenue, as broad, and about double the length of the mall at St. James's.   The houſe itſelf has nothing extraordinary in its appearance; but the gardens are as fine as gardens planned in the Dutch taſte, and formed on ground perfectly level, can be.   The orangery is reckoned equal to any in Europe.   Here is a kind of rural theatre, where plays may be acted during the fine weather.   There is a ſpacious amphitheatre cut out in green ſeats for

the

the spectators; a stage in the same taste, with rows of trees for side-scenes, and a great number of arbours and summer-rooms, surrounded by lofty hedges, for the actors to retire and dress in.

When the theatre is illuminated, which is always done when masquerades are given, it must have a very fine effect. The groves, arbours, and labyrinths, seem admirably calculated for all the purposes of this amusement.

In these gardens are several large reservoirs and fountains, and on one side, a canal above a quarter of a mile in length. I have not seen the famous jet d'eau, as the water-works have not been played off since I came to Hanover. On the whole, we pass our time very agreeably here. We have dined twice with Baron de Lenth, who has the chief direction of the affairs of this electorate, and at his house have met with the principal inhabitants. I make one of Marshal Sporken's party every night

at

at Whift, and pafs moft of my time in the fociety at his houfe.

The Duke of Hamilton having promifed to meet fome company at Brunfwick by a certain day, we fhall fet out for that place to-morrow—but have engaged to pay another vifit to Hanover before we go to Berlin.—My next therefore will be from Brunfwick, or poffibly from this place after our return.

L E T T E R LX.

WE remained a week at Brunſwick, and returned to this town about ten days ago. None of the family are there at preſent, except the Duke and Ducheſs, and the young Princeſs, their daughter.

The character of the Sovereign, at every court, has great influence in forming the taſte and manners of courtiers. This muſt operate with increaſed force in the little courts of Germany, where the parties are brought nearer to each other, and ſpend the moſt part of their time together. The pleaſure which the Ducheſs of Brunſwick takes in ſtudy, has made reading very faſhionable among the ladies of that Court: of this her Royal Highneſs gave me a cu-

‡   rious

rious inſtance the laſt time I had the honour of feeing her.

A lady, whoſe education had been neglected in her youth, and who had arrived
at a very ripe age without perceiving any
inconveniency from the accident, had obtained, by the intereſt of ſome of her rela-
tions, a place at the Court of Brunſwick.
She had not been long there, till ſhe perceived that the converſation in the Duchefs's
apartments frequently turned on ſubjects of
which ſhe was entirely ignorant, and that
thoſe ladies had moſt of her Royal Highnefs's ear, who were beſt acquainted with
books. She regretted, for the firſt time,
the neglect of her own education; and although ſhe had hitherto confidered that
kind of knowledge, which is derived from
reading, as unbecoming a woman of quality, yet, as it was now faſhionable at Court,
ſhe reſolved to ſtudy hard, that ſhe might
get to the top of the mode as faſt as poſſible.

She

She mentioned this refolution to the Duchefs, defiring, at the fame time, that her Highnefs would lend her a book to begin. The Duchefs applauded her defign, and promifed to fend her one of the ufefulleft books in her library—It was a French and German dictionary. Some days after, her Highnefs enquired how fhe relifhed the book. Infinitely, replied this ftudious lady.—It is the moft delightful book I ever faw.—The fentences are all fhort, and eafily underftood, and the letters charmingly arranged in ranks, like foldiers on the parade; whereas, in fome other books which I have feen, they are mingled together in a confufed manner, like a mere mob, fo that it is no pleafure to look at them, and very difficult to know what they mean. But I am no longer furprifed, added fhe, at the fatisfaction your Royal Highnefs takes in ftudy.

Since our return to Hanover, we have dined twice at the Palace. There is a houfehold

MANNERS IN FRANCE, &c. 97

household eftablifhed with officers and fervants, and the guard is regularly mounted,
as at the time when the Electors refided
here conftantly. The liveries of the pages
and fervants are the fame with thofe worn
by the King's domeftic fervants at St.
James's. Strangers of diftinction are entertained at the Palace in a very magnificent
manner. The firft of the entertainments I
faw was given to the Duke of Hamilton,
and the other to young Prince George of
Heffe Darmftadt, who arrived here a few
days fince, with Prince Erncft and Prince
Charles of Mecklenburg, brothers to the
Queen of Great Britain, both of whom are
in the Hanoverian fervice.

Moft of my time is fpent, as formerly,
at Marfhal Sporken's. The converfation of
a man of fenfe, who has been fifty years in
the fervice, and in high rank during a confiderable part of that time, which led him
into an intimacy with fome of the moft celebrated characters of the age, you may be

VOL. II.   H   fure

fure is highly interefting. It affords me
fatisfaction to be informed from fuch au-
thority, of many tranfactions in the laft
war, the common accounts of which are
often different, and fometimes contradictory. The Marfhal's obfervations are fenfible and candid, and his manner of converfing unreferved. He ferved with the
late Marfhal Daun in the allied army, oppofed to Marfhal Saxe, in the war 1741,
and has many curious anecdotes illuftrating
the characters of fome of the commanders
who conducted the armies during that
memorable period. He has a very high
opinion of Duke Ferdinand's military character, and declares, that of all the Generals he ever ferved under, that Prince feemed
to him to have the beft talents for conducting an army. He fays, that as Prince
Ferdinand had feldom held councils of war,
or communicated to the Generals of his
army any more of his plans than they
were to execute, it was difficult for them

†

to

to form a juft opinion of his capacity, while they remained with the army immediately under his command; but that he (Marfhal Sporken) had fometimes commanded a detached army, which obliged the Prince to be more communicative, and afforded the Marfhal the ftrongeft proofs of the depth of his judgment. Above all things, he admired the perfpicuity of his written inftructions.——Thefe, he faid, were always accompanied with the moft accurate and minute defcription of the country through which he was to march, every village, rivulet, hollow, wood, or hill on the route, being diftinctly particularifed, and the moft judicious conjectures concerning the enemy's defigns added, with directions how to act in various probable emergencies.

Upon the whole, Marfhal Sporken feemed convinced that great part of the fuccefs of the allies, during the late war in Weftphalia, was owing to the forefight, pru-

dence,

dence, and fagacity of their General. One memorable event, however, which has been cited as the moft ftriking proof of all thefe, he imagined was not fo much owing to any of them, as to the perfonal valour of a few regiments, and the good conduct of fome inferior officers. The Marfhal added, that his praifes of Duke Ferdinand's military abilities did not proceed from private attachment, for he could claim no fhare in his friendfhip; on the contrary, a mifunderftanding had happened between them, on account of an incident at the fiege of Caffel, the particulars of which he recapitulated, and this mifunderftanding was of a nature never to be made up.

The liberal, candid fentiments of this venerable man carry conviction, and command efteem. He is refpected by people of all ranks, and liftened to like an oracle. In the fociety generally to be found at the Marfhal's, there are fome nearly of his own age, who formed the private parties

of

of George the Second, as often as he came to vifit his native country. The memory of that monarch is greatly venerated here. I have heard his contemporaries of this fo-ciety relate a thoufand little anecdotes con-cerning him, which at once evinced the good difpofition of the King, and their own gratitude. From thefe accounts it ap-peared, that he was naturally of a very fo-ciable temper, and entirely laid afide, when at Hanover, the ftate and referve which he retained in England, living in that familiar and confidential manner which Princes, as well as peafants, will affume in the com-pany of thofe they love, and who love them.

Not only the perfonal friends of that monarch fpeak of him with regard; the fame fentiments prevail among all ranks of people in the Electorate. Nothing does more honour to his character, or can be a lefs equivocal proof of his equity, than his having governed thefe fubjects, over whom he had an unlimited power, with as much

juftice

juftice and moderation as thofe whofe rights are guarded by law, and a jealous conftitution.

The two vifits I have made to Hanover, have confirmed the favourable impreffion I had before received of the German character. One of the moft difagreeable circumftances which attend travelling is, the being obliged to leave acquaintances after you have difcovered their worth, and acquired fome degree of their friendfhip. As the feafon for the Pruffian reviews now approaches, we have already taken leave of our friends, and are to fet out to-morrow morning on our return to Brunfwick, that after remaining a few days there, we may ftill get to Potfdam in proper time.

I fhall not leave behind me every valuable acquaintance I have acquired fince I came to Hanover.—We met, on our laft arrival here, with Mr. Fortefcue, fon of Lord Fortefcue. He has been of our parties ever fince, and will accompany us to Brunfwick and Potfdam.

LETTER LXI.

Potſdam.

ON returning to Brunſwick, we found the Hereditary Princeſs had come from Zell a few days before, having left the Queen of Denmark in perfect health. The Princeſs reſided with her children at Antoncttenruche, a villa a few miles from Brunſwick. She invited the Duke of Hamilton, Mr. Forteſcue, and me, to dine with her the day before we were to ſet out for Potſdam. That morning I chanced to take a very early walk in the gardens of the palace.—The Duke of Brunſwick was there.—He informed me, that an expreſs had arrived with news of the Queen of Denmark's death.—They had received accounts a few days before that ſhe had been ſeized with a putrid fever.—He ſaid that

H 4   nobody

nobody in the town or court knew of this
except his own family, and defired that I
would not mention it to the Princefs,
who, he knew, would be greatly affected;
for he intended to fend a perfon, after her
company fhould be gone, who would inform her of this event, with all its circumftances.

When we went, we found the Princefs
in fome anxiety about her fifter;—yet
rather elated with the accounts fhe had received that day by the poft. She fhowed
us her letters.—They contained a general
defcription of the fymptoms, and conveyed fome hopes of the Queen's recovery.
Unable to bear the idea of her fifter's death,
fhe wrefted every expreffion into the moft
favourable fenfe, and the company met her
wifhes, by confirming the interpretation
fhe gave. To me, who knew the truth,
this fcene was affecting and painful.

As we returned to Brunfwick in the
evening, we met the gentleman who was
com-

commiffioned by the Duke to impart the news of the Queen's death to her fifter.—— We fupped the fame night at court, and took leave of this illuftrious family.—The Duchefs gave me a letter to her fon, Prince Frederick, at Berlin, which fhe faid would fecure me a good reception at that capital.

On coming to the inn, we found a very numerous company, and the whole houfe refounded with mufic and dancing. It is cuftomary all over Germany, after a marriage of citizens, to give the wedding-feaft at an inn. As there was no great chance of our being much refrefhed by fleep that night, inftead of going to bed, we ordered poft-horfes, and left Brunfwick about three in the morning.

· We arrived the fame afternoon at Magdeburg. The country all the way is perfectly level. The Duchy of Magdeburg produces fine cattle, and a confiderable quantity of corn, thofe parts which are not
marfhy,

marſhy, and over-grown with wood, being very fertile. I have ſeen few or no incloſures in this, or any part of Germany, except ſuch as ſurround the gardens or parks of Princes.

The King of Pruſſia has a ſeat in the diet of the empire, as Duke of Magdeburg. The capital, which bears the ſame name with the duchy, is a very conſiderable town, well-built and ſtrongly fortified. There are manufactories here of cotton and linen goods, of ſtockings, gloves, and tobacco; but the principal are thoſe of woollen and ſilk.

The German woollen cloths are, in general, much inferior to the Engliſh and French. The Pruſſian officers, however, aſſert, that the dark blue cloth made here, and in other parts of the King of Pruſſia's dominions, though coarſer, wears better, and has a more decent appearance when long worn, than the fineſt cloth manufactured in England or France.—Thus much

is

is certain, that the Pruffian blue is preferable to any other cloth made in Germany —The town of Magdeburg is happily fituated for trade, having an eafy com-
munication with Hamburg by the Elbe,
and lying on the road betweeen Upper and
Lower Germany. It is alfo the ftrongeft
place belonging to his Pruffian Majefty,
and where his principal magazines and
founderies are eftablifhed. In time of war,
it is the repofitory of whatever he finds neceffary to place out of the reach of fudden
infult.

Places where any extraordinary event
has happened, even though they fhould
have nothing elfe to diftinguifh them, intereft me more than the moft flourifhing
country, or fineft town which has never
been the fcene of any thing memorable.
Fancy, awakened by the view of the
former, inftantly gives fhape and features
to men we have never feen.—We hear
them fpeak, and fee them act; the paffions

are

are excited, the mind amufed ; the houfes,
the rivers, the fields around fupplying the
abfence of the poet and hiftorian, and re-
ftoring with new energy the whole fcene
to the mind.

While croffing the Elbe at this town
with the Duke of Hamilton, I recalled to
his memory the dreadful tragedy which
was acted here by the Auftrian General
Tilly, who, having taken this town by
ftorm, delivered up the citizens, without
diftinction of age or fex, to the barbarity
and luft of his foldiers. Befides the general maffacre, they exhibited fuch acts of
wanton cruelty, as difgrace human nature.
We viewed, with a lively fympathy, that
part of the river where three or four hundred of the inhabitants got over and made
their efcape :—all that were faved out of
twenty thoufand citizens!

This fad cataftrophe fupplied us with
converfation for great part of this day's
journey. It is unneceffary to comment on
an

an event of this kind to a perfon of the Duke's fenfibility.—Proper reflections arife fpontaneoufly in a well-formed mind from the fimple narrative.

The country is well cultivated, and fertile, for about two leagues beyond Magde-burg; afterwards it becomes more barren, and within a few leagues of Brandenburg, it is as naked and fandy as the deferts of Arabia.

Brandenburg, from which the whole Electorate takes it name, is but a fmall town, divided into Old and New by a river, which feparates the fort from both. The principal trade is carried on by fome French woollen manufacturers, whom the King has encouraged to refide at this town. The whole number of inhabitants does not amount to more than 1500.

On entering the Pruffian garrifon towns, you are ftopped at the gate; the officer of the guard afks your name, whence you come,

come, whither you are going ? and takes your anſwers down in writing. This is done in the French garriſons alſo, but not with the ſame degree of form and accuracy.

When the title of Duke is given, the guard generally turns out under arms. As for Milord, it is a title treated with very little ceremony, either in France or Germany. It is often aſſumed in foreign countries by thoſe who have no right to it, and given to every Engliſhman of a decent appearance. But Duke, in Germany, implies a Sovereign, and is more reſpectable than Prince. Every ſon of a Duke in this country, is called Prince, although he had as many as old King Priam.

We arrived laſt night at Potſdam, which important piece of news, you will pleaſe to obſerve, I have taken the earlieſt opportunity of communicating.

LETTER LXII.

Potfdam.

THE day after our arrival here, I waited on the Count Finkenftein, and defired to know when the Duke of Hamilton
and I could have the honour of being prefented to the King, requefting, at the fame
time, the liberty of attending at the reviews. I was not a little furprifed when
this minifter told me, that I muft write a
letter to his Majefty, informing him of
that requeft, and that I fhould certainly receive an anfwer the day following. It appeared very fingular to write to fo great a
Prince upon an affair of fuch fmall importance; but the Count told me this was the
eftablifhed rule. So I immediately did as
I was defired.

Next

Next morning one of the court-fervants called for me at the inn, and delivered a fcaled letter addreffed to me, and figned by the King, importing, that as the court would foon be at Berlin, the minif- ter in waiting there would let the Duke of Hamilton and Mr. Moore know when they might be prefented, and that they were very welcome to attend at all the reviews.

In the evening we were prefented to the Prince and Princefs of Pruffia, who refide almoft conftantly at Potfdam. He is a tall, ftout-made, handfome man, of about thirty-five years of age. The Princefs is of the family of Heffe-Darmftadt, and has a great refemblance to her aunt, whom we had feen at Carlfruche. We have had the honour of fupping with them twice during the few days we have been at Potfdam.

The Prince and all the officers have been employed every morning in preparing for the

the reviews. Yefterday, for the fecond time, there were feven thoufand men reviewed by the King. The Prince of Pruffia's fon, a child of fix or feven years old, was prefent on foot with his tutor, and unattended by any officer or fervant. They mingled without any mark of diftinction among the other fpectators. I mentioned my furprife at this to the tutor. In France, faid he, it would be otherwife: the Dauphin, at the age of this child, would be carried to the review in a coach, with a troop of mufqueteers to attend him; but here, the King and Prince are equally defirous that their fucceffor fhould be brought up in a hardy manner, and without any ftrong impreffion of his own importance. Sentiments of that kind will come foon enough, in fpite of all the pains that can be taken to exclude them.

The troops were drawn up in one line along the fummits of fome hills. From this fituation they defcended over very

'unequal

unequal and rough ground, firing in grand
divifions all the way, till they came to the
plain, where they went through various
evolutions.   But as we were to fet out in a
little time for Berlin, where the grand reviews of that garrifon are to take place, I
fhall fay no more on the fubject of reviews
till then.

Our mornings, fince we came hither,
have always been paffed with the troops
in the field.   The forenoons we have fpent
in looking at every thing curious in the
town.   The houfes are built of a fine
white freeftone, almoft all of them new,
and nearly of the fame height.   The
ftreets are regular and well-paved, and
there are fome very magnificent public
buildings ; fo that Potfdam has every requifite to form an agreeable town, if by
that word is meant the ftreets, ftone-walls,
and external appearance.   But if a more
complex idea be annexed to the word, and
if it be thought to comprehend the finifh-

4   ing,

ing, furniture, and conveniencies within the houfes, in that cafe Potfdam is a very poor town indeed.

The King having expreffed a great in- clination to fee this town increafe, feveral monied people built houfes, partly to pay their court to his Majefty, and partly be- caufe, by letting them, they found they would receive very good intereft for their money. But as the town did not augment fo quickly as he wifhed, his Majefty or- dered feveral ftreets to be built at once, at his own expence. This immediately funk the value of houfes, and the firft builders found they had difpofed of their money very injudicioufly.

Towns generally are formed by degrees, as the inhabitants increafe in numbers; and houfes are built larger and more commo- dious as they increafe in riches; for men's ideas of conveniency enlarge with their wealth. But here the matter is reverfed;

I 2   the

the houfes are reared in the first place, in hopes that their fair outfides, like the nymphs of Circe, will allure travellers, and attract inhabitants. Hitherto their power of attraction has not been ftrong; for few towns are worfe inhabited than Potfdam, though the houfes are let to merchants and trades-people at very fmall rents.

I was not a little furprifed, while I walked through the town, to fee buff-belts, breeches, and waiftcoats, hanging to dry from the genteeleft looking houfes, till I was informed, that each houfekeeper has two or more foldiers quartered in his houfe, and their apartments are, for the moft part, on the firft floor, with windows to the ftreet; which I am told is alfo the cafe at Berlin. The King choofes that his foldiers fhould be quartered with the citizens, rather than in barracks. This ought to be a fufficient anfwer to thofe military gentlemen, who infift on building barracks for the foldiers in Britain, upon the

the fuppofition, that our army cannot be well difciplined without them. For it could fcarcely be expected, or wifhed, that the Britifh army were under more rigid difcipline than the Pruffian.

I imagine the Pruffian foldiers are quartered in private houfes rather than barracks, from confiderations diametrically oppofite to thofe which produce the fame effect in England.—The Britifh parliament have always fhown an averfion to lodging the military in barracks, and have preferred quartering them in the citizens' houfes, that a connection and good-will may be cultivated between the foldiers and their fellow-citizens; and that the former may not confider themfelves as a diftinct body of men, with a feparate intereft from the reft of the community, and whofe duty it is implicitly to obey the will of the crown at all times, and upon all occafions.

Whereas here it may not be thought expedient to lodge great bodies of armed

I 3   men.

men together in barracks, left they should, during the night, form combinations deſtructive of diſcipline, and dangerous to government. This cannot happen in the day-time, becauſe then the officers are preſent, and the ſoldiers are not allowed even to ſpeak to each other when under arms; and while off duty, their time is wholly filled up in cleaning their arms, accoutrements, and clothes, and preparing for the next guard.—I imagine theſe may be part, at leaſt, of the reaſons which induce the King of Pruſſia to prefer quartering his men in private houſes; for in all other reſpects, lodging them together in barracks would be more convenient, and more agreeable to the genius of his government.

The palace at Potſdam, or what they call the caſtle, is a very noble building, with magnificent gardens adjacent. I ſhall not trouble you with a deſcription of either, only it ſtruck me as a thing rather uncommon in a palace, to find the ſtudy by far

the

the fineſt apartment in it. The ornaments of this are of maſſy ſilver. The writing-deſk, the embelliſhments of the table, and the accommodations for the books, were all in fine taſte.

The perſon who attended us, aſked if we had any deſire to ſee his Majeſty's wardrobe?—On being anſwered in the affirmative, he conducted us to the chamber where the monarch's clothes are depoſited; it had a very different appearance from his library. The whole wardrobe conſiſted of two blue coats, faced with red, the lining of one a little torn;—two yellow waiſtcoats, a good deal foiled with Spaniſh ſnuff;—three pair of yellow breeches, and a ſuit of blue velvet, embroidered with ſilver, for grand occaſions.

I imagined at firſt, that the man had got a few of the King's old clothes, and kept them here to amuſe ſtrangers; but, upon enquiry, I was aſſured, that what I have mentioned, with two ſuits of uniform

I 4   which

which he has at Sans-Souci, form the entire wardrobe of the King of Pruffia. Our attendant faid, he had never known it more complete. As for the velvet fuit, it was about ten years of age, and ftill enjoyed all the vigour of youth. Indeed, if the moths fpared it as much as his Majefty has done, it may laft the age of Methufalem.— In the fame room, are fome ftandards belonging to the cavalry. Inftead of the ufual fquare flag, two or three of thefe have the figures of eagles in carved filver fixed on a pole.

In the bed-chamber where the late King died, at the lower part of the window which looks into the garden, four panes have been removed, and a piece of glafs, equal in fize to all the four, fupplies their place. We were informed that his late Majefty's fupreme delight through life had been to fee his troops exercife, and that he had retained this paffion till his laft breath. When he was confined to his room by his

laft

laft illnefs, he ufed to fit and view them through the window, which had been framed in this manner, that he might enjoy thefe dying contemplations with the greater conveniency. Becoming gradually weaker, by the increafing diftemper, he could not fit, but was obliged to lie on a couch through the day. When at any time he was uncommonly languid, they raifed his head to the window, and a fight of the men under arms was perceived to operate like a cordial, and revive his fpirits.—By frequent repetition, however, even this cordial loft its effect.—His eyes became dim—when his head was raifed, he could no longer perceive the foldiers, and he expired.

This was feeling the ruling paffion as ftrong in death as any man ever felt it.

LETTER LXIII.

Potſdam.

I Have been twice or thrice at Sans-Souci, which is at a ſmall diſtance from Potſdam. The King lives conſtantly at the Old Palace, except when ſome people of very great diſtinction come to reſide with him for ſome days. He then receives them at the New Palace, and remains there him-ſelf during their ſtay.

The gallery contains a great collection of paintings, ſome of them originals, high-ly eſteemed.—The moſt valuable are of the Flemiſh ſchool.—Some people who paſs for connoiſſeurs, and for aught I know may be what they pretend, aſſert, that the King has not a juſt taſte in painting, which appears by his purchaſing a great many

very

very indifferent pictures. Whatever may be in that, it is certain that his Majesty does not give the least importance to the opinion of these connoisseurs; but buys, admires, and avows his admiration of such pieces as appear excellent in his own eyes, without regarding what they or others may think. It has no weight with him, that the piece is said to be by Raphael, Guido, or Corregio. If he see no beauty in it, he says so, and without ceremony prefers the work of a modern or obscure painter.

This is considered by many critics in painting as blasphemy, and shocks them more than any other species of impiety. A painter and great connoisseur, whom the King had disgusted, by rejecting some pictures of his recommending, and by purchasing others which he had condemned, said (speaking of the King), The man imagines, because he can play on the German flute, and has been praised by a par-

cel

cel of poets and philofophers, and has gained ten or a dozen battles, that therefore he underftands painting; but fighting battles is one thing, and a true knowledge of painting is another, and that he will find to his coft.

A few years after the late war, the King of Pruffia began to build the new palace of Sans-Souci, which is now completely finifhed, and is certainly a very noble and fplendid work. The offices are at a confiderable diftance, and are joined to the body of the palace by a double colonnade, which has a very grand effect. The front of the palace feems rather crowded, by the great number of ftatues which are intended to ornament it. Thefe are generally in groups, reprefenting fome ftory from Ovid. This building has a cupola, terminated by a large crown, fupported by the three Graces. The Duke of Hamilton obferved, that three Pruffian grenadiers would have been more fuitable. On the ground-floor,

in

in the middle, there is a large hall, whofe floor, fides, and roof, are all of marble. It is called the grotto, and the ornaments correfpond with that name. This room can be agreeable only when the weather is exceffively hot. In Italy it would be de-lightful. The roof of this hall is low, and vaulted, and fupports another room in all refpects of the fame dimenfions, only higher. This fecond room is alfo lined with beautiful marble. The other apart-ments are adorned with rich furniture and paintings, all very fhowy. Many people think them gaudy.—It muft be owned, that the gilding is laid on with a very lavifh hand.

Oppofite to the old palace of Sans-Souci, and immediately without the gardens, Lord Marechal has built a houfe, where he conftantly refides. You are well ac-quainted with the amiable character of this nobleman. We waited on him foon after our arrival, and have dined with him feveral

veral times fince. On the front of his houfe is this infcription:

FREDERICUS II. NOBIS HÆC OTIA FECIT.

Adjoining to this houfe is a fmall garden, with a door which, communicates with the King's garden of Sans-Souci, fo that his Lordfhip has the full enjoyment of thefe gardens. The King has alfo a key to my Lord's little garden, and frequently walks by this paffage to vifit him.

We fet out for Berlin to-morrow. Adieu.

LETTER LXIV.

Berlin.

WE arrived here in the height of the preparation for the reviews. Nothing was to be feen in the ftreets but foldiers parading, and officers hurrying backwards and forwards. The town looked more like the cantonment of a great army, than the capital of a kingdom in the time of profound peace. The Court itfelf refembled the levee of a General in the field —except the foreign minifters, and a few ftrangers, every man there (for there were no women) was dreffed in a military uniform.

Mr. Harris, the Britifh minifter, attended the Duke of Hamilton the day we were prefented to the King. A fon of Prince Kaunitz's,

Kaunitz's, and fome other ftrangers, were prefented at the fame time. The Count Reufe, chamberlain of the Court, named each perfon to his Majefty as he approach-ed. He converfed a confiderable time with the Duke, and fpoke a few words to every perfon who was prefented.—His countenance and manner are exceedingly animated.—He feemed that day in very high fpirits, and fpoke to all his officers in an eafy ftyle, and with a kind of gay affa-bility. On their part, they appear before their mafter with an erect military bold-nefs, free from that cringing addrefs which prevails in many Courts, but would not fucceed here.

The King was three days at Berlin be-fore the reviews began, and paffed fome hours every morning in the park, where there were four or five thoufand men or-dered daily, not to be exercifed, but fim-ply that the King might examine the ftate of each corps in particular: and it is incre-dible

dible with what accuracy and minute attention he did examine them, the Colonel
of the regiment under fcrutiny walking
along with him, to anfwer any queftion,
and hear his directions and remarks. By
this exactnefs, he not only knows the condition of the army in general, but the appearance, degree of difcipline, and ftrength
of each regiment.

The whole number reviewed was about
thirty-fix or thirty-eight thoufand, confifting of the garrifon of Berlin, and troops
from fome of the adjacent towns and villages. This army was in the field three
mornings fucceffively, and the operations
were different each day. I fhall endeavour
to give you an idea of the plan of the laft
day's review, which is frefheft in my memory.

At break of day, about eight thoufand
men marched out of Berlin, under the
command of a general officer, and took
poffeffion of a village, fituated on a rifing

ground, at the diſtance of two or three miles. About an hour after, the King himſelf joined the army, which was aſſembled without the gates. He divided it into three columns. Two general officers took the command of two of them; he himſelf led the third. The whole marched by three different routes towards the village, where the former detachment had now taken poſt. In the attack and defence of this village the review conſiſted.

As the army advanced, they were cannonaded from the village, but could not be ſuppoſed to ſuffer much, becauſe the leader of each column advanced with caution, taking ſuch circuits as expoſed the men very little.

At length rhe three columns met on a large plain near the village, but protected from the batteries by a riſing of the ground. Here the King formed the army into two lines. While this was doing, they were perfectly ſecure; but they could

8 not

not advance towards the village otherwife
than by going over the fwell in the ground,
and being expofed to all the cannon of the
enemy.   This was to be performed, therefore, with as much expedition as could be
confiftent with good order.   The right
wing of the army made the attack.   As
foon as the fignal was given, all the drums
and fifes ftruck up at once.   The foldiers
advanced with a rapid pace.   A numerous
train of large field pieces, placed at proper
intervals, advanced with equal velocity,
and kept in a line with the front rank.
The rapidity with which they were charged
and difcharged, as they advanced, was quite
aftonifhing.   When the line came within
a proper diftance of the village, the foldiers began to ufe their firelocks.   In the
mean time there was a furious cannonade,
and difcharge of fmall fhot from the village.   The King was between the advancing line and the village during the attack.
When they had got very near the hedges,

a new

a new battery opened from the village. The King gave a fignal, and the firft line broke, fell into an artificial confufion, and gave back towards the fecond line, which opened at feveral places, and clofed again the moment the retreating line had pierced through. The fecond line then moved to the attack, as the former had done. This alfo feemed to be repulfed—a retreat was founded, and the whole wing began to retire. A body of cavalry then appeared from the village, and were advancing to charge the retreating army, but were themfelves charged, and driven back, by the cavalry of the right wing.

A body of huffars purfued alfo from the village, and haraffed the retreating army. Thefe were fometimes repulfed by the foldiers, who turned and fired on them, and fometimes by detached parties of cavalry, which drove them away.

Thefe

Thefe various operations lafted from five in the morning till noon, when the troops returned to Berlin.—It is hardly poffible for any words of mine to convey an adequate idea of the perfect manner in which thefe evolutions were executed. The charges made by the cavalry were praifed by the King himfelf. I had never feen fo great a body together, and had no idea that it was poffible to charge at full gallop, and keep the ranks and diftances fo exactly as they did.

Upon the principle, that velocity is equal to weight, they endeavour to compenfate for the lightnefs of the horfes by the quicknefs of their motion. The huffars in the Pruffian army are taught, not only to harafs a retreating army in detached parties, but to charge like heavy cavalry in a large body. The late General Seidlitz, who had the reputation of being the beft officer of cavalry in Europe, brought the Pruffian dragoons to a wonderful de-

gree

gree of perfection, and it is said that he gained the battle of Rofbach by one brisk charge. Ever since, the King of Pruffia has beftowed great attention on his cavalry. They are now habituated to charge in large bodies, and at full fpeed.

The cuiraffiers are the flower of the Pruffian army. They are dreffed in buff coats, and wear very heavy iron breaft-plates, which cover all the fore-part of the body, and have been tried by mufket-fhot before they are delivered to the men.

I neglected to mention, that the infantry were ordered to fhout as they advanced to the attack on the village, and that this practice is adopted by the Pruffians in actual fervice. The King, as I am informed, is of opinion, that this keeps up the fpirits of the men, and prevents them from reflect-ing on the danger of their fituation. There are a greater proportion of drummers in the Pruffian fervice than in moft others: a regua regulation, in all probability, founded on the fame principle.

The evening after the reviews, there were a concert and fupper at Prince Henry's palace. The Queen was prefent, and the King's brothers, Henry himfelf, and Ferdinand, with their Princeffes; alfo the Prince and Princefs of Pruffia, Prince Frederick of Brunfwick and his Princefs, and a numerous company. I here delivered to Prince Frederick the letter I had brought from his mother, who I found had before apprized him of my intention to go to Berlin.

The King himfelf was not prefent. He feldom appears at feftivals. All his hours, not employed in bufinefs, he fpends in reading, or in the fociety of a few people whom he efteems. The Hereditary Prince of Brunfwick is at prefent the King's moft conftant companion, a choice which does not more honour to the Prince than to the King's difcernment.

K 4 · Prince

Prince Henry's palace is one of the moft magnificent buildings in Berlin. No fubject of the King of Pruffia lives in a more fumptuous manner than this Prince, who keeps a numerous eftablifhment of fervants, moftly handfome young men, very richly dreffed. The entertainment on this occa- fion was remarkably fplendid.

LETTER LXV.

Berlin.

THE day after the reviews, the King, attended by his nephew, the Prince of Pruſſia, and the Hereditary Prince of Brunſ-wick, ſet out for Magdeburg, where there is a camp of 15,000 men. He afterwards will proceed to Sileſia, and his new ac-quired dominions in Poland, and is not ex-pected at Potſdam for ſix weeks at leaſt.

His Majeſty makes the ſame circuit twice every year.—Surely no King in Eu-rope can have ſuch a thorough knowledge of his dominions and ſubjects as this mo-narch.—His abſence from Berlin has made but little relaxation in the duty, and none in the diſcipline, of the troops. The re-

views

views were fcarcely over, when field-days began. There are 1500 or 2000 of the troops belonging to this garrifon, exercifed in the park almoft every morning, befides thofe who appear on the parade for the ordinary guards.

A review, fuch as that which I endeavoured to defcribe, is undoubtedly one of the fineft fhows that can be exhibited: but when a fpectator of fenfibility reflects on the means by which thefe poor fellows are brought to this wonderful degree of accuracy, he will pay a fevere tax for this fplendid exhibition.—The Pruffian difcipline on a general view is beautiful; in detail it is fhocking.

When the young ruftic is brought to the regiment, he is at firft treated with a degree of gentlenefs; he is inftructed by words only how to walk, and to hold up his head, and to carry his firelock, and he is not punifhed, though he fhould not fuc-

ceed

ceed in his earlieſt attempts:—they allow his natural awkwardneſs and timidity to wear off by degrees:—they ſeem cautious of confounding him at the beginning, or driving him to deſpair, and take care not to pour all the terrors of their diſcipline upon his aſtoniſhed ſenſes at once. When he has been a little familiariſed to his new ſtate, he is taught the exerciſe of the fire-lock, firſt alone, and afterwards with two or three of his companions. This is not entruſted to a corporal or ſerjeant; it is the duty of a ſubaltern officer. In the park at Berlin, every morning may be ſeen the Lieutenants of the different regiments exerciſing, with the greateſt aſſiduity, ſometimes a ſingle man, at other times three or four together; and now, if the young recruit ſhows neglect or remiſſneſs, his attention is rouſed by the officer's cane, which is applied with augmenting energy, till he has acquired the full command of his fire-
lock.

lock.—He is taught fteadinefs under arms, and the immobility of a ftatue;—he is informed, that all his members are to move only at the word of command, and not at his own pleafure:—that fpeaking, coughing, fneezing, are all unpardonable crimes; and when the poor lad is accomplifhed to their mind, they give him to underftand, that now it is perfectly known what he can do, and therefore the fmalleft deficiency will be punifhed with rigour. And although he fhould deftine every moment of his time, and all his attention, to cleaning, his arms, taking care of his clothes, and practifing the manual exercife, it is but barely poffible for him to efcape punifh-ment; and if his captain happens to be of a capricious or cruel difpofition, the ill-fated foldier lofes the poor chance of that poffibility.

As for the officers, they are not indeed fubjected to corporal punifhment, but
they

they are obliged to beſtow as unremitting attention on duty as the men. The ſubalterns are almoſt conſtantly on guard, or exerciſing the recruits: the Captain knows, that he will be blamed by his Colonel, and can expeĉt no promotion, if his company be not as perfeĉt as the others: the Colonel entirely loſes the King's favour if his regiment ſhould fail in any particular: the General is anſwerable for the diſcipline of the brigade, or garriſon, under his immediate command. The King will not be ſatisfied with the General's report on that ſubjeĉt, but muſt examine every thing himſelf; ſo that from his Majeſty, down to the common centinel, every individual is alert. And as the King, who is the chief ſpring and primum mobile of the whole, never relaxes, the faculties of every ſubordinate perſon are kept in conſtant exertion: the conſequence of which is, that the Pruſſian army is the beſt diſciplined, and the readieſt for ſervice at a minute's warning, of any

now

now in the world, or perhaps that ever was in it. Other monarchs have attempted to carry difcipline to the fame degree of perfection, and have begun this plan with aftonifhing eagernefs. But a little time and new objects have blunted their keennefs, and divided their attention. They have then delegated the execution to a commander in chief, he to another of inferior rank, and thus a certain degree of relaxation having once taken place, foon pervades the whole fyftem; but the perfeverance of the King of Pruffia is without example, and is perhaps the moft remarkable part of his extraordinary character.

That degree of exertion which a man of a vigorous mind is capable of making on fome very important occafion, the King of Pruffia has made for thirty years at a ftretch, without permitting pleafure, indolence, difguft, or difappointment, to interrupt his plan for a fingle day.—And he has obliged every perfon through the various

rious departments of his government to make, as far as their characters and strength could go, the same exertions.—I leave you to judge in what manner such a man muft be ferved, and what he is capable of performing.

LETTER. LXVI.

Berlin.

NO condition in life can be more active, and at the same time have less variety in it, than that of a Prussian officer in the time of peace. He is continually employed in the same occupation, and continually occupied in the same place. There is no rotation of the troops as in the British service. The regiments which were placed in Berlin, Magdeburg, Schweidnitz, and the other garrisons at the conclusion of the war, remain there still. It is dreaded, that if they were occasionally moved from one garrison to another, the foreigners in the service, who are exceedingly prone to desertion, might then find opportunities, which according to the present plan they cannot: for however desirous a Prussian

soldier

foldier may be to defert, the thing is almoft impoffible. The moment a man is
miffing, a certain number of cannons are
fired, which announce the defertion to the
whole country. The peafants have a confiderable reward for feizing a deferter, and
are liable to fevere penalties if they harbour, or aid him in making his efcape, and
parties from the garrifons are fent after
him in every direction.

As none of the foldiers are ever allowed
to go without the walls of the town, it requires great addrefs to get over this firft
difficulty; and when they have been fo far
fortunate, many chances remain againft
their efcaping through the Pruffian dominions; and even when they arrive fafe in
any of the neighbouring ftates,

Nunc eadem fortuna viros tot cafibus actos
 Infequitur *.

* The fame fate awaits them there, after all the dan-
gers they have efcaped.

For there they will probably be obliged to inlift again as foldiers; fo that on the whole, however unhappy they may be, it is abfurd to attempt defertion in any other way than by killing themfelves, which method, as I am told, begins to prevail.

In confequence of their remaining conftantly in the fame place, converfing always with the fame people, and being employed uniformly in the fame bufinefs, the Pruffian officers acquire a ftaid, ferious appearance, exceedingly different from the gay, diffipated, degagé air of Britifh or French officers. Their only amufement, or relaxation from the duties of their profeffion, feems to be walking on the parade, and converfing with each other. The inferior officers, thus deprived of opportunities of mixing in general fociety, and not having time for ftudy, can have no very extenfive range of ideas. Their knowledge, it muft be confeffed, is pretty much confined to that branch of tactics in which

they

they are fo much employed; and many of them at length feem to think, that to ftand firm and fteady, to march erect, to wheel to the right and left, and to charge and difcharge a firelock, if not the fole ufe of human creatures, is at leaft the chief end of their creation.

The King, as I have been informed, has no inclination that they fhould reafon on a larger compafs of thought, which might poffibly lead them to defpife their daily employment of drilling foldiers, counting the buttons of their coats, and examining the ftate of their fpatterdafhes and breeches. For as foon as men's minds become fuperior to their bufinefs, the bufi-nefs will not be fo well performed. Some application to other ftudies, and opportunities of mixing with a more general fo-ciety, might make them more agreeable men, but not better captains, lieutenants, and adjutants.

His

His Majefty imagines he will always find a fufficient number of men of a more liberal turn of mind, and more extenfive notions, for officers of great truft and feparate commands, where the general muft act according to emergencies, and the light of his own underftanding. He believes alfo, that this general fyftem will not deprive him of the advantage of particular exceptions, or prevent genius from being diftinguifhed, when it exifts in the humbleft fpheres of his fervice. As often, therefore, as he obferves any dawnings of this kind; when any officer, or even foldier, difcovers uncommon talents, or an extenfive capacity, he is fure to be advanced, and placed in a fituation where his abilities may have a full power of exertion; while thofe muft ftand ftill, or be moved by a very flow gradation, who have no other merit to depend on for promotion but affiduity alone, which, in the Pruffian fervice, can never conduct

to

to that rank in the army, where other qua-
lifications are wanted.

As to the common men, the leading
idea of the Pruffian difcipline is to reduce
them, in many refpects, to the nature of
machines ; that they may have no volition
of their own, but be actuated folely by
that of their officers ; that they may have
fuch a fuperlative dread of thofe officers as
annihilates all fear of the enemy; and that
they may move forwards when ordered,
without deeper reafoning or more concern
than the firelocks they carry along with
them.

Confidering the length to which this
fyftem is carried, it were to be wifhed
that it could be carried ftill further, and
that thofe unhappy men, while they retained the faculties of hearing and obey-
ing orders, could be deprived of every
other kind of feeling.

The common ftate of flavery in Afia,
or that to which people of civil profef-

L 3   fions

fions in the moft defpotic countries are fubject, is freedom in comparifon of this kind of military flavery. The former are not continually under the eyes of their tyrants, but for long intervals of time may enjoy life without reftraint, and as their tafte dictates; but all the foreign foldiers in this fervice, and thofe of the natives, who are fufpected of any intention to defert, and confequently never allowed furloughs, are always under the eye of fomebody, who has the power, and too often the inclination, to controul every action of their bodies, and every defire of their hearts.

Since fuch a number of men all over Europe are doomed to this ftate of conftraint, it is much to be lamented that, from the nature of the fervice, the doom fhould fall on the ufeful, induftrious peafantry, who, when uncontrolled by cruel and abfurd policy, pafs their days in cheerfulnefs, tafting every real pleafure without the

the naufea of fatiety, or the ftings of remorfe, and perhaps, of all mankind, have
the greateft enjoyment of life. The fum-
total of happinefs, deftroyed by removing
men from this fituation into a ftate of mifery, muft be infinitely greater than if
many of the ufelefs, wealthy, and luxu-
rious could be tranflated into the fame
ftate. This would not be annihilating
happinefs, but only fhifting the fcene of
the wretched. Such recruits would only
be haraffed by the caprices of others inftead of their own;—plagued with the
manual exercife, inftead of being tortured
by peevifhnefs and difguft;—laid up in
confequence of running the gantlet, inftead of being laid up with the gout;—
and, finally, knocked down by a cannon-
ball, inftead of being killed by a fit of the
apoplexy or a furfeit.

L 4

LETTER LXVII.

Berlin.

INSTEAD of troubling you with any more obfervations of my own, on the nature of the Pruffian difcipline, or the principles on which it is founded, I fhall give you the fubftance of fome converfa_ tions I have had on that fubject with a Pruffian officer of character.

Walking one morning in the park, we faw a poor fellow fmartly caned, for no other reafon, but becaufe he did not return the ram-rod into his piece with fo much celerity as the reft of the platoon. I turned away with indignation from the fight, which the officer obferving, faid, You think the punifhment too fevere for the crime!—There was no crime, faid I: the

the ram-rod flipt through his fingers by accident, and it is not poffible to imagine, that the man had any intention to perform this important motion lefs rapidly than his comrades. Every thing muft be confidered as of importance by a foldier, replied my Pruffian acquaintance, which his officer orders him to do. In all probability, the fault was involuntary ; but it is not always poffible to diftinguifh involuntary faults from thofe that happen through negligence. To prevent any man from hoping that his negligence will be forgiven as involuntary, all blunders are punifhed, from whatever caufe they happen ; the confequence of which is, that every man is more attentive and alert than he would otherwife be. I remember, added he, that it was very ufual on field-days for the dragoons to have their hats blown off. Nobody fufpeƈted that they had bribed the wind to play this trick ; yet a general officer being put out of humour by the frequency of the accident,

accident, gave orders to punish every man to whom it should happen; and since that order was put in force, the hats have been much seldomer blown off.

I then mentioned a fact which appeared to me still more extraordinary. A huffar, at the last review, had fallen from his horse at full gallop, and was so much bruised, that it was found necessary to carry him to the hospital; and I had been assured, that as soon as the man should be perfectly recovered, he would certainly be punished for having fallen. Now, continued I, though a man may be a little careless about his hat, it cannot be imagined, that this huffar was not seriously inclined to keep his seat; for by falling, he might have broke his neck, or have been trod to death: Or, even if you choose to suppose that he did not ride with all the attention he ought, yet, as he received one severe punishment by the fall, it would be cruel to inflict another. I have nothing to oppose to the

solidity

folidity of your argument, replied the Pruffian, but that General Seidlitz, who was the
beft officer of cavalry in the world, firft
introduced this piece of cruelty, fince
which it is certain, that the men have
not fallen fo often. The King imagines,
continued the Pruffian, that difcipline is
the foul of an army; that men in the different nations of Europe are, in thofe
qualities which are thought neceffary for
a foldier, nearly on a par; that in two
armies of equal numbers, the degrees of
difcipline will determine how far one is
fuperior to the other. His great object,
therefore, is to keep his own army at the
higheft poffible degree of perfection in this
effential point. If that could be done by
gentle means, undoubtedly he would prefer them.—He is not naturally of a cruel
difpofition.—His general conduct to officers
of rank proves this.—Finding that the
hopes of promotion, and a fenfe of honour, are fufficient motives to prompt
them

them to their duty, he never has had recourfe, except in cafes of treachery, to
any higher punifhment than difmiffing
them. In fome remarkable inftances, he
has difplayed more mildnefs than is ufual
in any other fervice. Some of his Generals have allowed towns of the greateft importance to be taken by furprife; others
have loft intire armies; yet he never was
influenced by popular clamour, or by the
ruinous condition of his own affairs in
confequence of thofe loffes, to put any of
the unfortunate generals to death. And
when any of them have been fufpended
for a certain time, or declared, by the
decree of a court-martial, incapable of a
military command under him, he has never aggravated the fentence by any oppro-
brious commentary, but has rather al-
leviated it by fome claufe or meffage,
which fpared the honour of the condemned
general.

The

The common foldiers cannot be kept to their duty by mild treatment. Severe and immediate corporal punifhment is found abfolutely neceffary.—Not to ufe it at all, or to ufe it in a degree incapable of producing the full effect, would be weaknefs. Soldiers are fometimes punifh-ed for flips, which perhaps all their at-tention cannot prevent ; becaufe, though it is impoffible to afcertain, that any par-ticular man could have avoided them, yet experience has taught, that, by punifhing every blunder, fewer are committed on the whole. This fufficiently juftifies the practice of what you call cruelty, but which is in reality falutary difcipline ; for an individual fuffering unjuftly is not fo great an evil in an army, as the permit-ting negligence to pafs unpunifhed. To allow ten guilty men to efcape, rather than rifk the punifhment of one innocent perfon, may be a good maxim in morality, or in civil government, but the reverfe will be found preferable in military difcipline.

When

When the Pruffian had finifhed his difcourfe, I faid, You feem to neglect all
thofe incitements which are fuppofed to
influence the minds of foldiers; the love
of glory, the love of country, you count
as nothing. You addrefs yourfelf to no
paffion but one.—Fear is the only inftrument by which you compel your common
men to deeds of intrepidity.—Never mind
the inftrument, replied the Pruffian, but
look to the effect.

I am convinced, anfwered I, that Britifh
foldiers, with that degree of difcipline
which fubfifts in our army, which is not
near fo rigid as yours, animated by their
native courage, and the intereft which even
the common men take in all their country's quarrels, are at leaft equal to any other
troops.

I hope, faid he, the experiment will
not be made foon, for I efteem your nation, and fhould be forry to fee your troops
oppofed

oppofed to ours in the field : but till they are, you cannot be fure of the juftnefs of your affertion.   The advantages you gained over the French in the late war rather makes for my argument, becaufe the French army is more remifs in the article of difcipline than yours.

I then returned to my old ground, the cruelty of haraffing and tormenting men without intermiffion; and afferted, that the advantages arifing from fuch exceffive feverity, even thoygh they fhould be as great as he reprefented, could not form a fufficient reafon for rendering the lives of fo many men miferable.

I do not know that they are miferable, replied he.—When men are but indifferently fed, forced to perform very hard duty, certain of being feverely punifhed for the fmalleft faults, and fometimes even for their misfortunes, can you doubt, faid I, that thefe men are miferable ?—They do

not

not feem miferable, replied he, they bear it very well.——And would you, added I, have the lefs remorfe in tormenting men, becaufe they have the ftrength of mind to bear it well?

I then told him a ftory I had heard of an Englifh failor, who was tried for a rob- bery he had committed on the highway. While his doom was pronouncing, he raif- ed a piece of rolled tobacco to his mouth, and held it between his teeth till he heard the fentence of death paffed on him. He then bit off a piece of the tobacco, and be- gan to chew it with great unconcern. Sirrah, faid the judge, piqued at the man's indifference, do you know that you are to be hanged in a very fhort time?—So I hear, faid the failor, fquirting a little to- bacco juice from his mouth.—Do you know, rejoined the judge, where you will go when you die?—I cannot tell indeed, an't pleafe your honour, faid the failor.——

Why,

Why, then, cried the judge, with a tre-
mendous voice, I will tell you: You will
go to hell, you villain, and there be burnt
to all eternity.—If I ſhould, replied the
ſailor, with perfect tranquillity, I hope,
my Lord, I ſhall be able to bear it.

LETTER LXVIII.

Berlin,

BERLIN is certainly one of the moſt beautiful cities in Europe. The ſtreets are built in a very regular manner, and of a commodious breadth. In the new town they are perfectly ſtraight. Frederick-ſtreet is reckoned two Engliſh miles and a half, or a French league, in length. Others, which go off at right angles from that, are a mile, or a mile and a half long.

Some people aſſert, that Berlin covers as much ground as Paris. Theſe are not Frenchmen, as you will readily believe; neither am I of that opinion, but it certainly approaches much nearer to Paris in ſize than in number of inhabitants; Berlin is undoubtedly more than half the ſize

of

of Paris, yet I am convinced it does not contain above a fifth of the inhabitants.

There are a few very magnificent buildings in this town. The reft are neat houfes, built of a fine white free-ftone, generally one, or at moft two ftories high. Here, as at Potfdam, the finifhing within does not correfpond with the elegance of the outfide, and the foldiers are quartered on the ground-floor in rooms looking to the ftreet. The principal edifices are the King's palace, and that of Prince Henry. Both of thefe are very magnificent. The arfenal, which is a noble ftructure, is built in the form of a fquare. We were informed, that at prefent it contains arms for 200,000 men. I am convinced this is no exaggeration.

The new Roman Catholic church is by far the moft elegant place of worfhip in the city. The King allows the free exercife of every religion over all his dominions. He thinks the fmalleft controul over men's

M 2   confciences

confciences highly unjuft. He even has
the delicacy not to influence them by his
example, and offends no religion, by giving a preference to any one in particular.

On the front of the opera-houfe, which
is a very beautiful ftructure, is this infcription :

FREDERICUS REX, APOLLINI ET MUSIS.

After obferving the infcriptions and ornaments of the palaces and other public
buildings, the new method of decorating
the churches, the number of Mercuries,
Apollos, Minervas, and Cupids, that are
to be met with in this country, a ftranger
might be led to fufpect, that the Chriftian
religion was exploded from the Pruffian
dominions, and old Jupiter and his family
reftored to their ancient honours.

There is an equeftrian ftatue of William,
the Great Elector, on the new bridge over
the Spree. This is highly efteemed as a
piece of fine workmanfhip.—In the corner

of

of one of the fquares, is a ftatue of Marfhal
Schwerin. He is reprefented holding the
enfign with which he advanced at the
famous battle of Prague.—Perceiving his
troops on the point of giving way, he
feized this from the officer's hands whofe
duty it was to carry it, and marched towards the enemy, calling out, Let all but
cowards follow me. The troops, afhamed
to abandon their general, charged once
more, and turned the fortune of the day.—
But the brave old Marfhal was killed, in
the eighty-fourth year of his age.—Do not
you think the trouble of living fo long was
amply repaid by fuch a death ?

Inftead of faints or crucifixes, the King
intends, that the churches of Berlin fhall
be ornamented with the portraits of men
who have been ufeful to the ftate. Thofe
of the Marfhals Schwerin, Keith, Winter-
field, and fome others, are already placed
in the great Lutheran church.

M 3   The

The fociety into which ftrangers may be admitted in this capital, is not various or extenfive. The Pruffian officers of the higher ranks, whofe time is not entirely engroffed, like that of their inferiors, by the duties of their profeffion, live moftly with their own families, or with each other. Exclufive of other reafons which might determine them to this, it is underftood, that the King does not approve of their forming intimacies with foreign minifters, or with ftrangers.

The Duke of Hamilton followed the King to Magdeburg to fee the reviews there, and has fince made a tour as far as Leipfic, with two Englifh gentlemen. My connection with him, and the letter I brought from the Duchefs of Brunfwick, have procured me invitations, which I fhould otherwife have had but a fmall chance of receiving. I paffed a day lately at a very pleafant villa, about fix miles from Berlin, belonging to the King's brother, Prince Ferdinand.

Ferdinand. He is married to a fifter of the Princefs of Heffe Caffel's. The Princefs of Pruffia was there at the fame time, and Prince Frederick of Brunfwick with his Princefs, who is remarkably pretty. I have the honour of fupping fometimes with Prince Frederick, who lives conftantly at Berlin. To the fpirit and vivacity common to all his family, he adds a tafte for poetry, and has compofed fome dramatic pieces in the French language, which have been reprefented on a little theatre in his own houfe, and in private focieties at Berlin.—There has been a continued round of feafting all the laft week.

The Princefs of Pruffia gave a breakfaft at a garden in the Park, to which a large company was invited. There was dancing, which continued all the forenoon. Upon all thefe occafions, I faw none of that ftate and ceremony of which the Germans are accufed. Thofe of the higheft rank behaved with the greateft eafe and affability

M 4   to

to every perfon prefent, and joined in the country-dances, without obferving any form or etiquette.

The minifter, Count Finkenftein, gave a great dinner and ball, on account of the marriage of one of his fons. The Count Reufe, and fome others, have alfo given entertainments; but the chief and permanent fociety is to be found at the houfes of the foreign minifters who refide here. I have been introduced to all of them by Mr. Harris, his Majefty's envoy extraordinary, who lives here in a ftyle which does honour to his country and himfelf.

We have received very great civilities alfo from Baron Van Swieten, minifter from the Court of Vienna, a man of wit and erudition. He is fon to the celebrated phyfician, whofe works are fo highly efteemed all over Europe. There are two or three general officers who are pretty often at the houfes of thefe minifters, and entertain ftrangers occafionally at home.—
Befides

Befides thofe I have named, there are very
few of the King of Pruffia's fervants who
have any connection with the ftrangers that
come to Berlin. I have had the happinefs
of forming an acquaintance here with two
very agreeable French gentlemen, the
Marquis de Laval, fon of the Duke of
that name, and the Count de Clermont,
grandfon of that Monf. de Saint Hillaire,
whofe arm was carried off by the fame
bullet which killed Marfhal Turenne.
You remember the fentiment which St.
Hillaire expreffed to his fon, who lamented his wound—A fentiment which proved,
that his magnanimity was equal to that of
the hero whom he fo greatly preferred to
himfelf.

Adieu.

LETTER LXIX.

Berlin.

WHEN we arrived here firſt, the Queen
lived at Mont Bijou, a ſmall palace
juſt without the gates. Her majeſty had
a public day twice a week while ſhe remained there ; but ſhe has lately removed
to Shoenhauſen, another palace, ſituated
two leagues from Berlin, where ſhe paſſes
the ſummer. Here ſhe has a public day
only once a week. The Princes, the nobility, the foreign miniſters, and ſtrangers,
generally attend on theſe occaſions at five
in the evening. After her Majeſty has
walked round the circle, and ſpoke a few
words to every one, ſhe ſits down to cards.
There is a table for the Queen, and one
for each of the Princeſſes, all of whom
chooſe their own parties. The reſt of the

company

company prefent themfelves for a few minutes at each of thefe card-tables, after
which the duty of the day is over, and
they walk in the garden, or form parties
at cards in the other apartments, as they
think proper, and return to Berlin when it
begins to grow dark. On fome particular
nights, her Majefty invites a confiderable
number of the company to fupper, who
then remain till midnight.

The Queen's Court refembles the other
Courts of Europe; whereas that at Sans-
Souci is upon quite a new plan. No
ftrangers are received there, nor any other
perfons, except fuch as have real bufinefs
with the King. There his Majefty is employed in his affairs from morning till evening, and fpends the hours he deftines for
relaxation in the company of two or three
men of letters, and a few officers, who
dine with him daily.—When he has bufinefs with any of his fervants, or with the
foreign minifters, which cannot be executed

ed by letter, they attend him at Sans-Souci, and come away as foon as that bufinefs is tranfacted.

Thofe affemblies at Shoenhaufen are the only eftablifhed amufement for the ladies of quality at Berlin during the fummer; but you have frequent opportunities of meeting with the court ladies at the houfes of the foreign minifters.

The French manners and turn of think- ing certainly prevail very little among the Pruffian officers; but the ladies of the court of Berlin have more the air of French women, than thofe of any court I have feen. Mademoifelle de Hartfield, firft lady of honour to the Queen, with an infinite deal of wit, has all the eafe and elegance which diftinguifh the ladies of the Court of Verfailles.

His Majefty very feldom appears at the Queen's court, or at any place where women form part of the affembly. When he inclines to unbend, his amufements are

of

of a nature in which they can take no ſhare. I once ſaid to a lady of this Court, that it was a pity his Majeſty did not love women.—Conſidering his time of life, ſaid ſhe, we could diſpenſe with his love ; but it is hard that he cannot endure us.

Notwithſtanding this humour of the King's, the ladies here are by no means neglected by the men in general. Many of the married women particularly, have avowed admirers, who attend them on all occaſions, are invited with them to all en-tertainments, ſit next them at table, and whom the maſter or miſtreſs of the feaſt takes care to place in the ſame party with them at cards. When a lady is not pro-vided with an attendant of this kind, her huſband, as well as herſelf, is generally a little out of countenance, and both ſeem rather in an awkward ſituation, till this neceſſary concomitant be found.

A misfortune of a very ſerious nature happened lately to a certain gentleman here ;

here; inftead of expreffing concern about him or his wife (for he was a married man), every body fympathized, in the tendereft manner, with another lady, between whom and this unfortunate gentleman the moft intimate connection was thought to fubfift: they faid fhe was one of the worthieft women in the world, and of fuch delicate feelings, that her health might be injured by the impreffion the gentleman's misfortune would make upon her mind—Being furprifed that no mention was made of his wife all this time, I afked if fhe might not alfo be in fome meafure affected by her hufband's difafter ?—I was told, that fhe was otherwife occupied, and that any thing which could happen to her hufband was of little or no importance to her. I then enquired if fhe and her hufband lived on bad terms; I was informed, that, on the contrary, they were on the beft footing in the world, for that he was much attached to another woman—(the very lady they fo

greatly

greatly lamented) and that his wife was entirely devoted to another man: fo the account between them being perfectly balanced, they lived free of all domeftic debates, in a ftate of mutual neglect, and engroffed with feparate paffions.

In this country, when both parties are willing, and when there are no children, a divorce may be obtained with very little trouble or expence; we are frequently in companies, where a lady, her prefent and former hufband, are at table, and all parties behave in the moft polite and friendly manner to each other.

I have heard of one gentleman, who having lived in a ftate of domeftic jarring with his wife, got her perfuaded to concur with him in applying for a divorce.— This was foon obtained.—He then married another woman, with whom he was violently in love, and expected, as ufual, eternal happinefs. After marriage, how-

ever,

ever, this paffion cooled rather fooner than common, and within a few months he became the profeffed admirer of his firft wife. He now faw a thoufand charms in her perfon and converfation, which had entirely efcaped his notice, while the bonds of wedlock fubfifted. He alfo difcovered, that certain peculiarities in her manner, which he had formerly thought exceedingly awkward, were in reality graceful. He expreffed his remorfe for his former blindnefs in the moft pathetic terms: the lady was foftened, and at length gave the moft perfect marks of forgivenefs; and it was univerfally thought, that he thus contrived to live in adultery with the very woman to whom he had been lawfully married.

Here jealoufy is held in equal contempt and deteftation, and fcandal is very little known. People feem fo fully occupied with their own private affairs, that they feldom

dom trouble their heads about the bufinefs of their neighbours. If, in the courfe of converfation, an intimacy of a particular kind is hinted at between people of different fexes, it is mentioned accidentally as a fact of no importance, and without the fmalleft blame or ill-natured reflection on either of the parties. One reafon of this may be, that there is fcarce fuch a thing (I am affured) as an old maid in his Pruffian Majefty's dominions.

The moft fashionable walk in Berlin, is in the middle of one of the principal ftreets. —Before the houfes on each fide there is a caufeway, and between thefe two caufeways are fine gravel walks, planted with lime-trees.—Tents are pitched under thefe, and ice, lemonade, and other refrefhments fold. The bands of mufic belonging to the regiments practife here in the fummer.—The company generally are in the greateft num‑ ber in the evening, and often walk till it is very late.

Vol. II.   N   ——Nunc J

————— Nunc et campus, et areæ,
Lenefque fub noctem fufurri,
Compofita repetantur hora *.

> * Beneath the grateful evening fhade,
>   The public walks, the public park,
> Are affignations duly made,
>   With gentle whifpers in the dark.

LETTER LXX.

Berlin.

NOTHING furprifed me more, when I firft came to Berlin, than the freedom with which the people fpoke of the meafures of government, and the conduct of the King. I have heard political topics, and others which I fhould have thought ftill more ticklifh, difcuffed here with as little ceremony as at a London coffee-houfe. The fame freedom appears in the bookfellers' fhops, where literary productions of all kinds are fold openly. The pamphlet lately publifhed on the divifion of Poland, wherein the King is very roughly treated, is to be had without difficulty, as well as other performances, which attack fome of the moft confpicuous characters with all the bitternefs of fatire.

N 2 A go-

A government, fupported by an army of 180,000 men, may fafely difregard the criticifms of a few fpeculative politicians, and the pen of the fatirift. While his Majefty retains the power of difpofing of the lives and properties of his fubjects as his wifdom fhall direct, he allows them the moft perfect freedom to amufe them-felves with as many remarks or jokes on his conduct as they pleafe.

The mind of this monarch is infinitely fuperior to that goffiping difpofition, by which the defpicable race of whifperers and retailers of fcandal thrive at fome courts. Convinced that the fame perfidy which can betray a real converfation, may invent a falfe one, he liftens to no little, malicious tales of what has paffed in pri-vate companies, or during the hours of convivial mirth. Any perfon who fhould attempt to repeat anecdotes of this kind to him, would be driven from his prefence with difgrace. He treats with equal con-tempt

4

tempt all anonymous letters, and every kind of injurious information, when the informer declines appearing openly in fupport of his affertions.

This great Prince is fo perfectly devoid of fufpicion and perfonal fear, that he refides at Sans-Souci without any guard whatever. An orderly ferjeant, or corporal only, attends there in the day-time to carry occafional orders to the garrifon at Potfdam, whither he always returns in the evening. In this houfe, where the King fleeps every night, there are not above ten or a dozen perfons, the fervants included. When you recollect that Sans-Souci is a folitary manfion, about half a league from Potfdam, where all the guards are fhut up, and therefore could be of no manner of ufe, in cafe of any attempt on the King's perfon during the night; when you confider that he, who lies thus defencelefs and expofed, is a defpotic monarch, who governs by the dictates of his

N 3 own

own will and underſtanding, without mind-
ing the ill-humour or diſcontent of any
man, or any ſet of men, and who, no
doubt, has many inveterate enemies, you
muſt confeſs, that all theſe circumſtances
argue great magnanimity.

Berlin, though not a fortified, is certainly a very military town. When all the
ſoldiers of the garriſon are preſent, they
amount to 30,000. In their general conduct
they are quiet, and the police of the town is
pretty well regulated. Yet there are ſome
kinds of irregularities which prevail in the
higheſt degree. Public courtezans are more
numerous here than in any town in Europe, in proportion to the number of inhabitants. They appear openly at the
windows in the day-time, becken to paſſen-
gers as they walk in the ſtreets, and ply
for employment in any way they pleaſe,
without diſturbance from the magiſtrate.

It

It feems to be a received opinion here, that the peace and happinefs of the community are not interrupted by this fpecies of licentioufnefs; or perhaps it is believed, that an attempt to reftrain it would be attended with confequences worfe than the thing itfelf. Therefore nobody is allowed to moleft or abufe thofe who have chofen this for a trade, and as little attention is paid to cuftomers, who frequent the chambers of thofe ladies, as if they ftept into any other houfe or fhop, to purchafe any other commodity.

Another fpecies of debauchery is faid to prevail in this capital.—I imagine, however, that what is related on that naufeous fubject is greatly exaggerated.

The better kind of citizens and manufacturers live entirely among thofe of their own rank, and without affecting the manners of the courtiers, or ftooping to the mean debauchery of the commonalty, main-

tain

tain the decency, plainnefs, and honefty of
the German character.

His Pruffian Majefty has applied his attention to no object with fo much zeal, and
fo little fuccefs, as to the eftablifhing of
commerce in his dominions. All his efforts, in order to this, have been rendered
abortive by injudicious taxes, by monopo-
lies, and other reftrictions. Commerce,
like the wild commoners of the air and the
foreft, when confined or fhackled, immediately droops and dwindles, or being
alarmed, like Love,

" ——————— at fight of human ties,
" Spreads its light wings, and in a moment flies."

LETTER LXXI.

Berlin.

I THANK you, Sir, for the poem and pamphlets you fent me by ——. I own I do not think the former a very capital performance; yet am not furprifed at the great run it has had. For though it, had contained ftill a fmaller proportion of wit, it would have been a good deal relifhed on account of the malignity and perfonal abufe with which it abounds.

The Englifh nation have always had a great appetite for political writings; but thofe who cater for them have of late ferved up fuch meffes of mere politics, as feem at length to have turned their ftomachs. A little wit or perfonal fatire is now found neceffary to make even a news-

paper

paper go down. The firſt is not always at the command of the caterer: he therefore uſes the other in its place, which anſwers his purpoſe as well.

I never had any delight in contemplating or expoſing the dark ſide of human nature; but there are ſome ſhades ſo obvious, that you cannot open your eyes without obſerving them. The ſatisfaction that many people enjoy in reading libels, wherein private characters are traduced, is of that number. If to be abuſed in pamphlets and news-papers is conſidered as adverſity, the truth of Rochefoucault's maxim is uncontrovertible:—Dans l'adverſité de nos meilleurs amis, nous trouvons toujours quelquechoſe qui ne nous déplait pas.

The common ſcribblers of the age have turned to their own account this malevolent diſpoſition, which they perceive to be ſo prevalent among men.—Like the

3   people

people who provide bulls and other animals to be baited by dogs for the amufement of the fpectators, thefe gentlemen turn out a few characters every week to be mangled and torn in the moft cruel manner in the public news-papers.

It is the favage tafte of thofe who pay for thefe amufements, which keeps them in ufe. The writers of fcurrilous books in London often bear no more malice to the individuals they abufe, than the people at Paris and Vienna, who provide the other horrid amufement, bear to the boars, bulls, and other animals which they expofe to the fury of dogs.

As for the fcribblers, they feldom have any knowledge of the perfons whofe characters they attack. It is far from being impoffible, that the author of the fevere verfes you fent me, has no more acquaintance with the lords and gentlemen againft whom he writes with fuch bitternefs, than

than the weaver who wove their pocket-handkerchiefs. The motive for the fabrication of the one as well as the other commodity moft probably was daily bread, and this poetafter has preferred fatire to panegyric, merely becaufe he knew the firft was moft to the tafte of his cuftomers.

I remember once to have been in a certain bookfeller's fhop, when a letter was delivered to him, inclofing a paper, which, after he had thrown his eyes over it, he prefented to me, telling me it was a character of Lord S——, which he intended to infert in a certain work then publifhing.—I fancy, added he, it will do pretty well; the author is a fharp blade, I affure you;—none of my boys carry fuch an edge, or cut fo deep, as that little gladiator.

I found this a moft bitter invective againft the above-mentioned nobleman, written with all the inveteracy of malice
and

and perfonal enmity, branding him as a prodigy of fenfuality, and accufing him of every villanous difpofition and propenfity that ever tainted the moft corrupt heart.

This, faid I, is a much more harmlefs production than is intended. The violence of this poifon will prove its own antidote. The moft voracious ftomach for flander and defamation will not be able to bear fuch a dofe, but muft reject it with difguft. Every reader of common underftanding will clearly perceive, that all this abufe has been dictated by malice and perfonal refentment.

Then, replied the bookfeller, every reader of common underftanding will clearly perceive what does not exift; for the writer of that paper, to my certain knowledge, never had the fmalleft intercourfe or connection with Lord S——; never bore him any ill-will, and has not the moft diftant wifh to injure that noble Lord; as a proof of of which, added he, taking another paper out of his drawer, here is a character of the fame nobleman, written by the fame author, which is to appear about a week after the publication of the former, by way of anfwer to it.

This fecond paper was a continued eulogium on Lord S—— from beginning to end, in which the *candid* author, having compared him to fome of the greateft and moft celebrated men, and having collected many of the brighteft flowers, with which Plutarch has adorned his worthies, he forms them into one large wreath, which he very ferioufly binds round the Englifh nobleman's brow, concluding with this obfervation, That as his Lordfhip refembled them in their virtues, fo like them he had been diftinguifhed by the moft virulent attacks of envy and malice, which was a tax that had always been paid for fuperior talents.

How

How comes my Lord S——, said I to the bookseller, to be selected from his brethren of the peerage, and distinguished so remarkably by the obloquy and the praise of your ingenious friend?

Because, replied he, that nobleman is at the head of an active department, and is one of those vigorous and decisive characters, which never fail to create a number of enemies and of friends. His enemies are delighted to see him abused, and it is expected, that his friends will be charmed to hear him praised; and, between the two, my friend's productions will find a brisk sale, and I hope to make a tolerable job of his Lordship; which, let me tell you, cannot be done with every man of rank.—Lord, Sir! there are some of them of such mawkish, water-gruel characters, as to interest no mortal. There is - - - - - - - - -, a man of such high rank and such a known name, that I thought something might have been made

of

of him:—And fo I employed my little Drawcanfir for and againft him, and two very pretty pamphlets he produced;—but juft as I was going to fend them to the prefs, I happened to fhew them to a friend of mine, who is an admirable judge in thefe matters.—Thefe pamphlets, fays he, are very well wrote; but they'll never pay the printing. The perfon who is the fubject of them is of fuch a cold, tame, civil, cautious difpofition, and has balanced fo exactly through the whole of his life, that he has never obliged or difobliged any one. He has neither friend nor foe in the world:—Every body fays, he is a good enough fort of a man ; but were he to break his neck to-night, no human creature would feel either forrow or fatisfaction at the event, and a fatire or panegyric on his grandmother would be as much read as thofe written on him.

In

In faith, Sir, concluded the Bookfeller, I took the hint, and fo the pamphlets never appeared.

. Though I was a good deal entertained with my friend the Bookfeller's reafoning, yet I could not help feeling indignation at the literary bravo, who lived in this infamous manner, by wounding and murdering, or at leaft attempting to murder, people's reputations. And thofe are not entirely free from blame, who, detefting the writer, take pleafure in the writings. He has very poffibly the plea of neceffitous circumftances to urge in alleviation of his wickednefs:—but the pleafure they take feems to proceed from a pure, difinterefted fondnefs of feeing others abufed. Many of thofe who cry fhame on the licentioufnefs of the prefs, and exclaim againft the injuftice and cruelty of tearing private characters to pieces in public papers, have the moft virulent of thefe productions ferved up every morning as regularly as their toaſt and butter.   If they would forego the pleaſure of reading the moſt malicious of thoſe compoſitions, the evil they complain of would ceaſe directly.

But it is ridiculous, and ſeems ungrateful, for people to affect an appearance of indignation againſt thoſe who provide for them one of the greateſt enjoyments of their lives.   To chuckle over ſcandal all the forenoon with every mark of pleaſure, and decry it in the evening with affected anger, is as prepoſterous as it would be in a judge, firſt to ſeduce a poor wench to fornication, and then puniſh her for the ſin.

You may poſſibly retort upon me, by putting me in mind of the admiration I expreſſed of the ſtyle of certain celebrated letters, wherein ſome eminent characters are diſſected, and tortured with the ſcientific ſkill of an anatomiſt, and the refined cruelty of an inquiſitor.   I anſwer, that I admired the wit and genius, but not the diſpoſition diſplayed in thoſe letters.

Malice,

Malice, when introduced by genius and wit, is often tolerated on account of the refpect due to the introducers; but when the wretch comes alone, or is accompanied by dulnefs, which often happens, fhe will be expelled with infamy from all good company.

Q 2

LETTER LXXII.

THE Pruffian army at prefent, according to my information, confifts of
180,000 men. If twenty, or even thirty
thoufand are deducted from this account,
on the fuppofition that it is exaggerated,
ftill the remainder will be very great;
and the expence of fuch an eftablifhment,
in time of peace, feems to many almoft incompatible with the King of Pruffia's refources. Although the revenues of this
monarch are much greater than is generally imagined, yet the armies he has fupported, and continues to fupport; the palace
he has built, and other expenfive undertakings which he has completed, are not
fuch proofs of the greatnefs of his revenue,
as of the prudence with which it has been
managed.

managed. Many other Princes have greater revenues, which, like water fpilt on uncultivated land, and affifting the growth of ufelefs weeds, are diffipated, without tafte or magnificence, on the trumpery of a court and their dependents. Perhaps it was never known what miracles œconomy and affiduity, through all the departments of government, could perform, till this monarch made it apparent.

In the King of Pruffia's dominions, there are none of thofe pofts which enrich individuals at the expence of the public; places fuited to the abilities and the luxury of the great, where the falary is large, becaufe the application and talents requifite are fmall. If thofe who hold the moft lucrative places in this court, can fupport a becoming dignity by the emoluments of their office, and lay up a very moderate provifion for their families, it is the utmoft they ever expect.

All

All commodities are highly taxed in the
Pruffian dominions. At Berlin, though
money is a great deal fcarcer than at London or Paris, a ftranger will find very little
difference in the ordinary expence of living.
There are no means by which his revenue
can be augmented, which this King has not
tried. He has taxed even the vanity of his
fubjects, and drawn confiderable fupplies
fince the beginning of his reign from that
plentiful fource. The rage which the Germans, above all men, have for titles,
prompts many of the wealthy citizens to
purchafe that of fome office about court;
and although the King employs no perfon
void of abilities, he never fcruples to permit this kind of traffic. The title, however, is literally all that is fold, for with regard to the real bufinefs of the office, the
purchafer has as little connection with
it after the bargain as before. Though
his Majefty fcarcely ever confults with
any body, he has more nominal privy-
counfellors

counfellors than any King in Chriften-
dom.

The taxes in general are invariably fixed;
but methods are found of drawing contri-
butions from the proprietors of the very
great eftates, which do not affect the
fmaller landlords, or the reft of the fubjects. The fpirit of the government is
not favourable to great and independent
Lords. But both the great and the fmall
landlords are prevented from fqueezing or
oppreffing the peafants. As the foldiery
are drawn from them, care is taken that
they fhall not be deprived of the chief
fource of health and vigour, and there is
no peafantry in Europe better fed than the
Pruffian.

The army is chiefly compofed of provincial regiments. The whole Pruffian
dominions being divided into circles or
cantons; in each of thefe, one or more regiments, in proportion to the fize and po-

O 4 puloufnefs

puloufnefs of the divifion, have been originally raifed, and from it the recruits continue to be taken; and each particular regiment is always quartered, in the time of
peace, near the canton from which its recruits are drawn.

Whatever number of fons a peafant may
have, they are all liable to be taken into
the fervice except one, who is left to affift
in the management of the farm.   The reft
wear badges from their childhood, to mark
that they are deftined to be foldiers, and
ready to ferve when the ftate requires them.
If a peafant has only one fon, he is not
forced into the fervice, except he has the
misfortune to be uncommonly ftout and
well-made.   The King, however, endeavours to fave his own peafantry, and draw
as many recruits as he can from other
countries:—For this purpofe, there are
Pruffian officers employed at Hamburgh,
Frankfort, and other free towns of Germany.   I have feen them alfo at Neufcha-
tel

tel, and at places near French garrifons, attempting to inlift men, and pick up deferters. The recruits procured in this manner, remain continually with the regiments in which they are placed; but the native Pruffians have every year eight or nine months of furlough, during which they return to their fathers' or brothers' houfes, and work at the bufinefs of the farm, or gain their livelihood in any other way they pleafe. Here is at once an immenfe faving in the expence of the army, and a great gain to the ftate from the labour of fo many men.

From this it appears, that the Pruffian army is neither more nor lefs than a ftanding militia, embodied for two or three months every year, and then difperfed to their ufual labours as farmers.

I think this decides our old difpute on the fubject of ftanding armies and militia. I expect therefore that you will, by the re-

turn

turn of poſt, fairly and candidly acknowledge that I was in the right, and that all
your arguments to prove, that a militia
could not be depended on in the time of
actual ſervice, are built on falſe principles,
and that my opinion was juſt and well-
founded.

Before cloſing this letter, I will inform
you of a very ſingular incident, the circumſtances of which I relate, not ſo much
with a deſign to illuſtrate the character or
ſentiments of the vulgar of this place in
particular, as to furniſh you with a curious
fact in the hiſtory of human nature in
general.

I went a few days ſince with Mr. Forteſcue
to ſee a man executed for the murder of a
child.—His motives for this horrid deed
were much more extraordinary, than the
action itſelf. He had accompanied ſome
of his companions to the houſe of a fellow
who aſſumed the character of a fortune-

teller,

teller, and having difobliged him, by expreffing a contempt of his art, the fellow,
out of revenge, prophefied, that this man
fhould die on a fcaffold.—This feemed to
make little impreffion at the time, but afterwards recurred often to this unhappy
creature's memory, and became every day
more troublefome to his imagination. At
length the idea haunted his mind fo in-
ceffantly, that he was rendered perfectly
miferable, and could no longer endure
life.

He would have put himfelf to death with
his own hands, had he not been deterred
by the notion, that God Almighty never
forgave fuicide; though, upon repentance,
he is very ready to pardon every other
crime. He refolved, therefore, to commit
murder, that he might be deprived of life
by the hands of juftice; and mingling a
fentiment of benevolence with the cruelty
of his intention, he reflected, that if he
murdered a grown perfon, he might poffibly

bly fend a foul to hell. To avoid this, he
determined to murder a child, who could
not have committed any fin which de-
ferved damnation, but dying in innocence,
would go immediately to Heaven. In
confequence of thefe ideas, he actually
murdered an infant of his mafter's, for
whom he had always fhewn an uncommon
degree of fondnefs. Such was the ftrange
account which this infatuated creature gave
on his trial;—and thus the random pro-
phecy proved, as in many other cafes, the
caufe of its own completion.

He was executed about two miles from
Berlin. As foon as he afcended the fcaffold,
he took off his coat and waiftcoat;—his
fhirt was rolled down below his fhoulders;
—his night-cap was pulled over his eyes;—
he was placed on his knees, and the executioner, with a fingle ftroke of a broad
fword, fevered his head from his body.—It
was the firft time this executioner had performed:—there were two others of the
fame

fame trade on the fcaffold, who exhibited an inftance of infenfibility more fhocking than the execution.—While the man's head rolled on the fcaffold, and the arteries of the trunk poured out their blood, thofe men, with the gayeft air you can imagine, fhook their brother by the hand, wifhed him joy, and clapped him on the back, congratulating him on the dexterous and effectual manner in which he had performed his office.

LETTER LXXIII.

THE Duke of Hamilton having expreffed an inclination to vifit the court of
Mecklenburg Strelitz, I accompanied him
thither foon after his return from Magdeburg and Leipfic.   The weather being ful-
try, his Grace thought that travelling in
the night would be moft agreeable.   We
did not fet out therefore till about fix or
feven in the evening,   The firft poft-houfe
is four German miles from Berlin; but as
great part of the road is through a large
wood, and the night became very dark,
the poftilions loft their way.   In a fhort
time we were perfectly bewildered, and
without the fmalleft notion which direction we fhould follow.   After many ineffectual attempts to find out the path, we

*   thought

thought it would be moſt prudent to un-
yoke the horſes, and allow them to graze
around, while we ſlept in the chaiſe till day-
break. This plan was literally followed:
as ſoon as the ſervants, by the light of the
riſing ſun, had diſcovered the path, we
proceeded by Oranienburg and Seidneek
to Reinſburg, which is a magnificent caſtle
belonging to Prince Henry of Pruſſia.

The gardens here are very extenſive, and
have been highly improved and ornamented by this Prince, who has a good taſte, and
a magnificent turn of mind.

When we arrived at the town of New
Strelitz, we were informed that the court
was at Brandenburg. The Ducal reſidence
was formerly at Old Strelitz; but the
palace there, with all the magnificent furniture and effects, was burnt to aſhes about
fifty years ago. The fire having broke out
in the night-time, the family themſelves
had a very narrow eſcape.

A new

A new palace has been fince built at the diftance of two Englifh miles from where the former ftood, but in a much more agreeable fituation, being placed on a gentle eminence near a fine lake; and the town of New Strelitz has gradually arifen in the neighbourhood.

After a fhort ftay at Strelitz, we proceeded to New Brandenburg, which is fome leagues farther north, and within a fmall diftance of the Baltic. We arrived there in the morning of the third day after we had left Berlin. When the Chamberlain of the Court was informed of the Duke of Hamilton's arrival, we received an invitation to dinner, and a coach and equipage were ordered to attend his Grace.

The reigning Duke of Mecklenburg Strelitz is unmarried, as well as the Princefs, his fifter, who lives conftantly with him. They are both of a darker complexion than the Queen of Great Britain, and

and neither of them fo tall; nor have they much external refemblance of her Majefty, except in the affability of their manner. The Duke is beloved by his fubjects, on account of the humanity and benevolence of his difpofition, which feem to be cha-racteriftic of the whole family.—After dinner there was a concert of mufic, and card-playing till fupper.

The whole country of Mecklenburg was for many centuries under the government of one Prince. In the year 1592, on the death of the Sovereign, it was divided be-tween his two fons. The eldeft retaining the Duchy of Mecklenburg Schwerin, which is confiderably the largeft fhare; the younger obtained the Duchy of Mecklen-burg Strelitz. This laft branch became extinct in the year 1695, and Duke Fre-deric William, of the eldeft branch, laid claim to the inheritance of the Duchy of Strelitz. But he was oppofed by Adolphus Frederic, his father's younger brother, and

the conteft was fettled by compromife between the parties in 1701. The right of
primogeniture, and the lineal fucceffion
were then eftablifhed in both houfes, and
this final agreement was ratified by the
Emperor.

The country here is not a fandy flat, as
around Berlin; but the foil becomes gradually better as you move from that city,
and around New Brandenburg it is remarkably fertile. Though the fouthern
border of this Duchy is flat, fandy, and barren, yet all the northern part is of a rich
verdure, finely diverfified with hills, meadows, woods, and feveral beautiful lakes,
from four to ten miles in length. The country yields plenty of corn, hemp, flax, excellent pafture for numerous flocks of fheep,
and a good breed of horfes.—New Brandenburg is a neat and thriving town, very
agreeably fituated. The inhabitants carry
on a confiderable trade in hops, which grow
in great abundance all around.

This

This country, which feems to be happy in its prince and other particulars, cannot rank among its bleffings the neighbourhood of fo great and warlike a monarch as the King of Pruffia. In the courfe of the late war, both the Mecklenburgs fuffered very feverely from this circumftance. The Ruffians and Auftrians, who pillaged the middle Mark of Brandenburg, did not afcertain with nicety where the King of Pruffia's dominions ended, and the Duke of Strelitz's began; but as often as there was any thing valuable to carry away, plundered both without diftinction. And when that Monarch himfelf was driven to extremity, and obliged to ufe every means of recruiting his army, the Mecklenburghers were cajoled and feduced by every art into the Pruffian fervice; and when thefe methods failed, they were, as it is faid, taken by force. Even at prefent, whenever the Pruffian recruiting officers know of a ftrong well-looking peafant belonging to the Duchy of Meck-

lenburg,

lenburg, they ufe every means they can devife to feduce him into their mafter's fervice.—Complaints are frequently made of thefe practices to his Pruffian Majefty, and redrefs will be given when it fhall pleafe the Lord.

The fecond day after our arrival, we fpent the forenoon in viewing every thing worthy of notice in the town, and dined again at court, where there was a more numerous company than had been the firft day. After dinner we accompanied his Highnefs and the Princefs to an affembly in the town, and returned to fup at the court. During fupper there was a concert of vocal and inftrumental mufic.

Having received every mark of polite attention from this Prince, we took leave of him and the Princefs, and left the town early, next morning, and returned by Old Strelitz, which is not in fuch a flourifhing condition, or fituated in fo fine a country, as

New

New Brandenburg.   While Britifh fubjects
pafs through this country, they will naturally reflect with gratitude and veneration
on the character of a Princefs whofe virtues
are an ornament to the Britifh throne, and
whofe amiable manners and prudent conduct have united the affections of a people
divided by party, and irreconcileable in fentiment on almoft every other fubject.

On our return to Berlin, I found a letter
from Lord Marechal, informing me, that
the King was expected at Potfdam within
a very few days; that great preparations
were making for the reception of the Princefs of Heffe and the Duchefs of Wurtemberg, who were then both at Berlin,
and were to pay a vifit to the King at
Sans-Souci; that they would be accompanied by the Princefs Amelia, the King's
unmarried fifter, and his two fifters-in-
law, for all of whom apartments were
preparing at the new palace, where his
majefty alfo was to refide all the time that

his illuſtrious gueſts ſhould remain. My Lord added, that the celebrated Le Kain, and a company of French comedians, were already arrived, and alſo a company of Italian actors and ſingers for the opera; and that both companies were to perform at the theatre within the palace; that a great concourſe of company was expected at Potſdam on the occaſion; that moſt of the apartments in the town were already beſpoke, and, as he imagined we ſhould incline to be there, he had engaged lodgings for us.

The Duke was extremely pleaſed with this obliging behaviour of Lord Marechal. I afterwards ſpoke to Mr. Harris on this ſubject, and enquired if he intended to be at Potſdam on the occaſion? He told me, that as the plays, operas, and other entertainments, were to be given in the palace, nobody could attend them except thoſe who had particular invitations; that neither he nor any of the foreign miniſters had been,

been, or, as he underſtood, were to be invited, nor did he hear that any ſtrangers
were expected;—and that he imagined it
would be unbecoming the Duke of Hamilton to be at Potſdam at that time, except
he could with propriety attend the entertainments at Sans-Souci.

His Grace, on hearing this account,
determined to remain here; but ſome days
after, I received a letter from Count Fin-
kenſtein, acquainting me, that he had orders to invite the Duke of Hamilton and me
to attend the entertainments to be given at
Sans-Souci. This afforded us great ſatiſ-
faction, not ſo much on account of the
public entertainments, as becauſe it will
give us opportunities, which we could not
otherwiſe have, of ſeeing the King of
Pruſſia, and probably in an eaſier way
than at Berlin. As for the uſual amuſements and ſplendour of courts, his Grace
diſplays more coolneſs about them than
one would naturally imagine, conſidering

the manner in which he is received, his time of life, and his perfonal appearance.

——Namque ipfa decoram
Cæfariem nato genitrix, lumenque juventæ
Purpureum, & lætos oculis afflârat honores.

Since our return from Mecklenburg, we have paffed our time almoft conftantly with Mr. Harris, who accompanied the Duke yefterday on his laft vifit to Shoen-haufen; for we fhall probably not return to this place from Potfdam. Mr. Fortefcue fet out a fews days ago for Frankfort on the Maine; his eafy humour, and original turn of thought, make his abfence felt with pain by all who have tafted the plea-fure of his converfation.

Adieu.

L E T T E R LXXIV.

W E have been here about a fortnight.
His Majeſty arrived at the new palace of Sans-Souci about the ſame time
that we came to Potſdam. The Princeſs
Amelia, who is miſtreſs of the ceremonies,
was there to receive him. The company
I formerly mentioned are all lodged in the
palace. I will give you a ſhort ſketch of
what has paſſed.

There has been a theatrical entertainment every ſecond or third day. His
Grace and I attend at Sans-Souci on
theſe days only. We drive from Potſdam
about five in the evening. The company
aſſemble in one of the apartments of the
palace about that time, and walk to the
play-

playhoufe a little before fix.   The theatre
is very well contrived for the accommodation of a fmall audience.   There are
neither boxes nor pit; but femicircular
benches in the front of the ftage.   The
foremoft bench is upon the floor;   the
others rife gradually behind, that all the
fpectators may fee equally well.

A few minutes after the company are
placed, the Royal Family arrive.   The
Princefs Amelia is led in by Prince Frederick of Brunfwick, and the Princefs of
Heffe by the King.   The Duchefs of
Wurtemberg, and the other Princeffes, are
led in after: they, and the ladies their
attendants, fit in the firft rows.   The
King generally feats himfelf in the third
or fourth.   The piece then begins, and
is ufually finifhed about nine, after which
all the company return to the large apartment, where the King remains converfing
in a familiar manner till fupper is ready.
He then retires, and goes to bed at ten.

S   Thofe

Thofe whom the Princefs Amelia orders to be invited, ftay to fupper; and there is generally a pretty numerous company.— We have been at this repaft three or four times, and ufually get to our lodgings at Potfdam about midnight.

Hitherto there have been no comedies acted, and I underftand there are to be none, becaufe Le Kain never acts in comedy; and for another reafon, which is equivalent to a thoufand,—his Majefty loves tragedy better.

Le Kain has already appeared in fome of his principal characters.—You need not doubt of his exerting all his powers before fuch an audience—I might have faid, fuch an auditor. The King feemed pleafed with his acting, and of confequence the courtiers were in raptures, and vied with each other who fhould praife him moft.

The tragedy of Oedipus is his Majefty's favourite piece. This has been reprefented twice, and he feemed to enjoy it very much

much on both occasions; particularly when the following speech against priests was pronounced:

> Tandis que par vos soins vous pouvez tout apprendre,
> Quel besoin que le Ciel ici se fasse entendre?
> Ces Dieux, dont le pontife a promis le secours,
> Dans leurs temples, Seigneur, n'habitent pas toujours;
> On ne voit point leur bras si prodigue en miracles;
> Ces antres, ces trépieds, qui rendent leur oracles,
> Ces organes d'airain que nos mains ont formés,
> Toujours d'un souffle pur ne font point animés.
> Ne nous endormons point sur la foi de leurs prêtres;
> Au pied du sanctuaire il est souvent des traîtres,
> Qui nous asservissant sous un pouvoir sacré,
> Font parler les destins, les font taire à leur gré.
> Voyez, examinez, avec un soin extrême,
> Philoctète, Phorbas, & Jocaste elle-même.
> Ne nous fions qu'à nous, voyons tout par nos yeux,
> Ce sont là nos trépieds, nos oracles, nos Dieux.

And afterwards, when Jocasta pours forth another tirade of the same kind, which terminates with these lines:

> Nos Prêtres ne font point ce qu'un vain peuple pense;
> Notre crédulité fait toute leur science;

I happened to sit next to the Abbé Bastiani, and, while the actress spoke this,

the

the king ftarted up, coughed, and laughed, with very fignificant geftures, to the eccle-fiaftic.

But though thefe paffages, and fome others, feem at firft fight to be fevere againft priefts, the tragedy of Oedipus, upon the whole, does them great honour. For all that is faid againft them, turns out to be unjuft, and it appears that the ora-cle, which had been treated in fuch fevere terms, was true, and that the high-prieft had acted throughout like an honeft and virtuous man. It furprifes me, therefore, that Voltaire fhould have taken the plot of his play from the Greek tragedy on this fubject, which has conftrained him, like Balaam the fon of Barak, to do honour to thofe whom he would have been better pleafed to have curfed.—And the King on his part (if I may prefume to fay it) could not have pitched upon a tragedy lefs à-pro-pos, if his intention was to turn the clergy into ridicule.

I have

I have no objection to this piece, on account of the honour done to the clergy; becaufe I cannot help forming an opinion of men from my own experience: And I have known fo many good men of that profeffion, that I fhould refpect it on their account, exclufive of other reafons.

But I own I have the misfortune not to follow this great monarch, and many other refpectable critics, in their admiration of the tragedy of Oedipus.—The fable, in my poor opinion, is too horrible.—The circumftance of Oedipus being married to his mother, and having children by her, is highly difgufting; and the idea it gives of Providence and the conduct of the gods, cannot have a good effect on the mind. Nothing could be more unjuft, than that Heaven fhould fend a plague among the inhabitants of Thebes, and pour fuch vengeance on poor Oedipus and Jocafta, for crimes of which it knew them to be innocent. We cannot help admitting the

juftice

juſtice of Oedipus's reproaches againſt the
gods, when he ſays,

Le voilà donc rempli cet oracle exécrable,
Dont ma crainte a preſſé l'effet inévitable :
Et je me vois enfin, par un mélange affreux,
Inceſte, & parricide, & pourtant vertueux.
Miſerable vertu, nom ſtérile & fûneſte,
Toi par qui j'ai réglé des jours que je déteſte,
A mon noir afcendant tu n'as pû reſiſter :
Je tombais dans le piége, en voulant l'éviter.
Un Dieu plus fort que moi m'entraînait vers le crime ;
Sous mes pas fugitifs il creuſait un abîme ;
Et j'etais, malgré moi, dans mon aveuglement,
D'un pouvoir inconnu l'efclave & l'inſtrument.
Voilà tous mes forfaits, je ne'en connais point d'autres.
Impitoyables Dieux, mes crimes ſont les vôtres,
Et vous m'en puniſſez . . . . .

We muſt fufpect, however, that Jocaſta
was miſtaken in the opinion ſhe utters in
the concluding lines of the tragedy.

Prêtres, & vous Thébains, qui futes mes ſujets,
Honorez mon bucher, & fongez à jamais,
Qu'au milieu des horreurs du deſtin qui m'opprime,
J'ai fait rougir les dieux, qui m'ont forcé au crime.

For thoſe, who could force innocent people
to commit criminal actions, and then puniſh

niſh them on that account, were not capable of bluſhing for any thing.

A French tragedy and Italian opera are
repreſented at this theatre alternately ; the
King attends the latter as punctually as
the former, and diſplays in his countenance that extreme ſenſibility to muſic,
which forms part of his character.   I imagine this Prince would ſucceed better in
any thing than in ſimulation, if he ſhould
ever think it worth his while to attempt
that part of hypocriſy,—his features are ſo
expreſſive of his feelings, that the firſt
would be conſtantly in danger of betray-
ing the other.   When there is no repre-
ſentation at the theatre, his Majeſty has
a private concert in his own apartment,
where he himſelf performs on the German
flute, in which inſtrument he has attained
the higheſt degree of excellence.—To theſe
concerts no ſtranger is admitted.

LETTER LXXV.

Potfdam.

WHEN we firft arrived here, there was nothing I was fo eager to fee as the Pruffian troops at their exercife; but the reviews at Berlin have completely fatiated my curiofity. And though the gardens of the palace are juft oppofite to the windows of our inn, I hardly ever go to look at the guards, who are paraded there every forenoon.—A few days ago, however, I happened to take a very early walk about a mile out of town, and feeing fome foldiers under arms, in a field at a fmall diftance from the road, I went towards them. An officer on horfeback, whom I took to be the Major, for he gave the word of command, was uncommonly active, and often rode among the ranks to

VOL. II.   Q   reprimand,

reprimand, or inftruct, the common men.
When I came nearer, I was much furprifed
to find that this was the King himfelf.
He had his fword drawn, and continued to
exercife the corps for an hour after. He
made them wheel, march, form the fquare,
and fire by divifions, and in platoons, obferving all their motions with infinite attention ; and, on account of fome blunder,
put two officers of the Prince of Pruffia's
regiment in arreft.—In fhort, he feemed to
exert himfelf with all the fpirit of a young
officer, eager to attract the notice of his
General by uncommon alertnefs.

I expreffed my furprife to an officer prefent, that the King was not willing to take
fome repofe, particularly from that kind
of employment of which he had had fo
very much of late, and that he could take
fo much pains with a mere handful of men
immediately after he had come from exercifing whole armies.

Ths

This gentleman told me, that, on this particular day, the King had been trying fome new evolutions; but though this had not been the cafe, he might very poffibly have been in the field:—for his maxim was, that his troops fhould difplay as much brifknefs on a common field-day as if they were to engage in battle; and therefore it was never known when he intended to be prefent, or when not:—that as for repofe, he took it between ten at night and four in the morning, and his other hours were all devoted to action, either of body or mind, or both; and that the exercife he had juft taken, was probably by way of relaxation after three hours previous labour in his cabinet.

The more I fee and hear of this extraordinary man, the more am I aftonifhed. He reconciles qualities which I ufed to think incompatible. I once was of opinion, that the mind, which ftoops to very fmall objects, is incapable of embracing great ones;

Q 2   —I am,

—I am now convinced, that he is an exception ; for while few objects are too great for his genius, none seem too small for his attention.

I once thought that a man of much vivacity was not capable of entering into the detail of bufinefs :—I now fee that he, who is certainly a man of wit, can continue methodically the neceffary routine of bufinefs, with the patience and perfeverance of the greateft dunce that ever drudged in a compting-houfe.

Since my laft, we have feen the Italians perform ; but neither the plays nor the operas, nor any part of the entertainments, intereft me half fo much, or could draw me fo affiduoufly to Sans-Souci, as the opportunity this attendance gives of feeing the King. Other monarchs acquire importance from their ftation; this Prince gives importance to his. The traveller in other countries has a wifh to fee the King, becaufe he admires the kingdom :—

here

here the object of curiofity is reverfed :—
and let us fuppofe the palaces, and the
towns, and the country, and the army of
Pruffia ever fo fine, yet your chief intereff
in them will arife from their belonging to
Frederic the Second ;—the man, who,
without an ally but Britain, repelled the
united force of Auftria, France, Ruffia,
and Sweden.

Count Neffelrode, talking with me on
this fubject, had an expreffion equally lively and juft: C'eft dans l'adverfité qu'il
brille, lorfqu'il eft bien comprimé il a un
reffort irréfiftible.

The evening of the day on which I had
feen the King in the field, I was at Sans-
Souci ; for I wifh to neglect no opportunity
of being prefent where this monarch is. I
like to ftand near him, to hear him fpeak,
and to obferve his movements, attitudes,
and moft indifferent actions. He always
behaves with particular affability to the
Duke of Hamilton. One evening, before

the

the play began, his Grace and I were standing accidentally with Count Finken-stein, in a room adjoining to the great apartment where the company were. The King entered alone, when he was not ex-pected, and immediately began a conver-fation with the Duke.

He afked feveral queftions relating to the Britifh conftitution; particularly at what age a peer could take his feat in parlia-ment?—When the Duke replied, At twenty-one—It is evident from that, faid the King, that the Englifh Patricians acquire the neceffary talents for legiflation much fooner than thofe of ancient Rome, who were not admitted into the Senate till the age of forty.

He then enquired about the ftate of Lord Chatham's health, and expreffed high efteem for the character of that minifter.—He afked me, if I had received letters by the laft poft, and if they mentioned any thing of the affairs in America? He faid,

there

there were accounts from Holland, that the Englifh troops had been driven from Bofton, and that the Americans were in poffeffion of that place.———I told him, our letters informed us, that the army had left Bofton to make an attack with more effect elfewhere.

He fmiled, and faid—If you will not allow the retreat to have been an affair of neceffity, you will at leaft admit, that it was *tout-à-fait à-propos.*

He faid he heard that fome Britifh officers had gone into the American fervice, and mentioned Colonel Lee, whom he had feen at his Court. He obferved, that it was a difficult thing to govern men by force at fuch a diftance; that if the Americans fhould be beat (which appeared a little problematical), ftill it would be next to impoffible to continue to draw from them a revenue by taxation; that if we intended conciliation with America, fome of our meafures were too rough; and if we in-

Q 4

tended

tended its fubjection, they were too gentle. He concluded by faying, *Enfin, Meſſieurs, je ne comprends pas ces choſes là; je n'ai point de colonie :—j'eſpère que vous vous tire- rez bien d'affaire, mais elle me paroit un peu épineuſe.*——Having faid this, he walked into the Princeſs's apartment, to lead her to the playhouſe, while we joined the company already aſſembled there.—The tragedy of Mahomet was performed, which, in my opinion, is the fineſt of all Voltaire's dramatic pieces, and that in which Le Kain appears to the greateſt advantage.

LETTER LXXVI.

Potſdam.

YOU expreſs ſuch an earneſt deſire to be made acquainted with every thing which regards the King of Pruſſia, that I am in danger of lengthening my deſcriptions with a tedious minutenefs. Yet I will riſk it, rather than give you reaſon to complain that I have not gratified your curioſity as fully as is in my power.

Do not imagine, however, that I preſume to draw a complete portrait of this monarch. That muſt be the work of much abler painters, who have ſeen him in a more familiar manner, and whoſe colours can give an expreſſion worthy of the original. I ſhall only attempt to give a faithful ſketch of ſuch features as I was

‡   able

able to feize during the tranfient views I myfelf had, or which I have learnt from thofe who have paffed with him many of the hours which he dedicates to free converfation, and the pleafures of the table.

The King of Pruffia is below the middle fize, well made, and remarkably active for his time of life. He has become hardy by exercife and a laborious life; for his conftitution originally feems to have been none of the ftrongeft. His look announces fpirit and penetration. He has fine blue eyes; and, in my opinion, his countenance upon the whole is agreeable. Some who have feen him are of a different opinion. All who judge from his portraits only, muft be fo; for although I have feen many which have a little refemblance of him, and fome which have a great deal, yet none of them do him juftice. His features acquire a wonderful degree of animation while he converfes.—This is entirely loft upon canvas.

He

He ftoops confiderably, and inclines his head almoft conftantly to one fide.

His tone of voice is the cleareft and moft agreeable in converfation I ever heard.

He fpeaks a great deal; yet thofe who hear him, regret that he does not fpeak a great deal more. His obfervations are always lively, very often juft, and few men poffefs the talent of repartee in greater perfection.

He hardly ever varies his drefs, which confifts of a blue coat, lined and faced with red, and a yellow waiftcoat and breeches. He always wears boots, with huffar tops, which fall in wrinkles about his ancles, and are oftener of a dark brown than a black colour.

His hat would be thought extravagantly large in England, though it is of the fize commonly ufed by the Pruffian officers of cavalry. He generally wears one of the large fide corners over his forehead and eyes, and the front cock at one fide.

He

He wears his hair cued behind, and dreſſed with a ſingle buckle on each ſide. From their being very careleſly put up and unequally powdered, we may natural- ly conclude, that the friſeur has been grately hurried in the execution of his office.

He uſes a very large gold ſnuff-box, the lid ornamented with diamonds, and takes an immoderate quantity of Spaniſh ſnuff, the marks of which very often appear on his waiſtcoat and breeches. Theſe are alſo liable to be ſoiled by the paws of two or three Italian greyhounds, which he often careſſes.

He dreſſes as ſoon as he gets up in the morning. This takes up but a few mi- nutes, and ſerves for the whole day.—You have often heard that the King of Pruſſia's hours from four or five in the morning, till ten at night, are all dedicated methodi- cally to particular occupations, either of buſineſs or amuſement. This is certainly
true;

true; and the arrangement has not fuf-tained fuch an interruption for many years, as fince the prefent company came to Potfdam.

Some who pretend to more than common penetration affert, that at prefent they can perceive marks of uneafinefs in his countenance, and feem convinced, that there will not be fuch another company at Sans-Souci during this reign.

All bufinefs with the King is tranfacted by letters. Every petition or propofal muft be made in this form, which is ad-hered to fo invariably, as I have been af-fured, that if any of his Generals wifhed to promote a cadet to the rank of an enfign, he would not venture to make his propofal in any other manner, even though he had daily opportunities of converfing with his Majefty.

The meaneft of his fubjects may apply to him in writing, and are fure of an anfwer. His firft bufinefs every morning

is

is the perufing the papers addreffed to him. A fingle word wrote with his pencil in the margin, indicates the anfwer to be given, which is afterwards made out in form by his fecretaries.—This method affords the King time to deliberate on the juftice and propriety of every demand, and prevents the poffibility of his being furprifed into a promife, which it might be inconvenient to perform.

He fits down to dinner precifely at noon. Of late he allows more time to this repaft than formerly. It is generally after three before he leaves the company. Eight or nine of his officers are commonly invited to dine with him. Since our coming to Potfdam, Count Neffelrode, and the Abbé Baftiani, two men of letters, were the only company, befides the officers, who dined with the King, while he lived in his ufual way at the Old Palace of Sans-Souci; and thofe two were then of his party almoft every day. The Count has now left this

Court;

Court; the Abbé has an apartment in the Palace. He is an Italian by birth, a man of wit, and an excellent companion.

At table, the King likes that every perfon fhould appear to be on a footing, and that the converfation fhould be carried on with perfect freedom. The thing, by the way, is impoffible. That confidential unreftrained flow of the heart, which takes place in a fociety of equals, is a pleafure which a defpotic Prince can never tafte. However, his Majefty defires that it may be fo, and they make the beft of it they can.

At one of thefe meetings, when the King was in a gay humour, he faid to Baftiani,—When you fhall obtain the tiara, which your exemplary piety muft one day procure you, how will you receive me when I arrive at Rome to pay my duty to your Holinefs ?—I will immediately give orders, replied the Abbé, with great readinefs, *Qu'on faffe entrer l'aigle noir,—qu'il*

me

me couvre de ses ailes, mais—qu'il m'épargne de son bec.

Nobody says more lively things in conversation than the King himself. Many of his bon mots are repeated here. I shall only mention one, which is at once an instance of his wit, and greatness of mind, in rendering justice to the merit of a man who has caused him more vexation than perhaps any other person alive.—When the King of Prussia had a personal meeting some years since with the Emperor; they always dined together, a certain number of their principal officers being with them. One day, General Laudohn was going to place himself at the bottom of the table, when the King, who was at the head, called to him, *Venez, je vous en prie, Monsieur Laudohn, placez vous ici. J'aime infiniment mieux vous avoir de mon côté que vis-à-vis.*

Though all the cordiality of friendship, and the full charms of unreserved society,

cannot

cannot exift where the fortune of every other individual depends on the will of one of the company ; yet the King endeavours to put every one as much at his eafe as the nature of the cafe will.admit, and I have heard of his bearing fome very fevere retorts with perfect good humour. He has too much wit himfelf, and is too fond of it in others, to repel its attacks with any other weapons than thofe which it, furnifhes. None but the moft abfurd of dunces could attempt to rally, without being able to allow of raillery ; and only the meaneft of fouls would think of revenging the liberties taken with a companion by the power of a King.

A very ftriking inftance of the freedom which may be ufed with him occurred a little before the late reviews, and what makes it more remarkable, it happened, not during the gaiety of the table, but on the very fcene of military ftrictnefs.

Two

Two regiments were in the field. That of General —— was one of them. This officer is fond of company, and paſſes more of his time in the ſociety of ſtrangers, and with the foreign miniſters, than moſt others in the Pruſſian ſervice.—Something, it is probable, had chagrined the King that morning. While the regiment advanced in a line, he ſaid to the General, who ſtood near him, Votre regiment n'eſt pas aligné, Monſieur ——, et ce n'eſt pas ſurprenant, vous jouez tant aux cartes. The General called out inſtantly with a loud voice to the regiment, Alte! and they immediately ſtopped: then, turning to the King, he ſaid, Il n'eſt pas queſtion, Sire, de mes cartes— Mais, ayez la bonté de regarder ſi ce regiment n'eſt pas aligné.—The regiment was in a very ſtraight line, and the King moved away without ſpeaking, and ſeemingly diſpleaſed, not with the General, but with himſelf.—This manly officer never had reaſon afterwards to believe that the King had taken his freedom amiſs.

I have

I have already faid, that it is abfolutely impoffible for any man to enjoy an office in the King of Pruffia's fervice without performing the duty of it. He is himfelf active and affiduous, and he makes it a point that all his minifters and fervants fhall be fo too. But to thofe who know their bufinefs, and perform it exactly, he is an eafy and equitable mafter.

A gentleman, who has been many years about his perfon, and is now one of his aid-de-camps, affured me of this:—The King underftands what ought to be done: and his fervants are never expofed to the ridiculous or contradictory orders of ignorance, or the mortifications of caprice.

His favourites, of whatever kind, never were able to acquire influence over him in any thing regarding bufinefs. Nobody ever knew better how to difcriminate the merit of thofe who ferve him in the important departments of ftate, from theirs who contribute to his amufement. A man

who

who performs the duty of his office with alertnefs and fidelity, has nothing to apprehend from the King's being fond of the company and converfation of his enemy. Let the one be regaled at the King's table every day, while the other never receives a fingle invitation; yet the real merit of both is known :—and if his adverfary fhould ever try to turn the King's favour to the purpofes of private hatred or malice, the attempt will be repelled with difdain, and the evil he intended to another, will fall on himfelf.

LETTER LXXVII.

Potsdam.

ON the days when there is no public court at Sans-Souci, we generally dine with Lord Marechal, who is always happy to fee the Duke of Hamilton, and is of great fervice to all Britifh fubjects while they remain here or at Berlin. Exclufive of other reafons he may have for efteeming the Duke, his Lordfhip evidently difplays a kind of partiality for his Grace, as the firft man in point of rank belonging to his country. This appears in a thoufand inftances; for with very liberal fentiments, and a moft benevolent heart, this venerable nobleman ftill retains a few Caledonian prejudices,

R 3

He

He afked one day of the Duke, If he reckoned himfelf a Scotchman? Moſt certainly I do, replied his Grace. By ſo doing you lie under a miſtake, ſaid my Lord; for I can aſſure you, and I am convinced the beſt lawyers in England will do the ſame, that you have a much juſter claim to all the privileges belonging to your Engliſh title of Brandon, though ſome of them, I fear, are ſtill diſputed.

It is to be hoped, ſaid the Duke, that the Houſe of Peers will not always refuſe to do my family juſtice; on a thorough examination of the caſe, I ſtill flatter myſelf they will grant me thoſe privileges, which have been, for no valid reaſons, refuſed my anceſtors. But in the mean time, why will your Lordſhip, more cruel than the Peers, deny my birth-right as a Scotchman?

Becauſe your birth gives you no ſuch right, replied the Earl; for you in reality

are

are but a North Briton :—unlefs your Grace
can prove that you were born before
the Union. But, continued he, with an
air of triumph, I am a real Scotchman:
—— —— ——adding a little after, with
a figh, and in a plaintive accent —— ——
and almoft the only one in the world ——
All the Scots of my acquaintance are now
dead.

The good old Earl is infinitely fond of
talking of his country, and of the days of
former years. When I make any enquiry
about the King of Pruffia, or concerning
Spain or Italy, in which country he refided fo long, he anfwers with a kind of
complaifant brevity, and immediately turns
the difcourfe back to Scotland, to which
his heart feems wonderfully attached.

In the time of dinner, one of his fervants, a ftout highlander, generally entertains the company by playing on the bag-
pipe. I have obferved, that thefe North

Britons

Britons (to abide by Lord Marechal's diftinction) who are the moſt zealous for
the intereſt and honour of their country,
and who value themſelves on being born
north of the Tweed, are particularly, if
not excluſively, fond of this inſtrument.
You will, at leaſt, allow that your gallant
friend, Lord Eglintoun, is no exception to
this obſervation; and perhaps you will admit, that it requires a conſiderable degree
of patriotiſm, or *amor Caledoniæ*, to have
a great reliſh for the melody of a bag-
pipe.

I called on Lord Marechal one afternoon, juſt as the King had left him: for
the monarch, without any form or previous notice, ſometimes walks through the
garden, and pays a ſhort viſit to his old
friend, to whom he has an unalterable
attachment, both from perſonal regard,
and on account of the high eſtimation in
which he holds the memory of his brother
Marechal Keith.

Another

Another day I was with the Earl, when
the Princeſſes of Pruſſia and Heſſe, with
Prince Frederic of Brunſwic, all entered and demanded coffee, which my
Lord immediately ordered, with the addition of a couple of melons; telling the
Princeſſes, he knew they would not ſtay
long enough with a man of eighty, to
give time for preparing a better repaſt.——
Thus favoured by the monarch and the
Princeſs, you will not doubt that the old
Earl's friendſhip is cultivated by the reſt of
the court.

The Hereditary Prince of Pruſſia lives
in a ſmall houſe in the town of Potſdam.
His appointments do not admit of that
degree of magnificence, which might be
expected in the Heir of the crown ;——but
he diſplays a ſpirit of hoſpitality far
more obliging than magnificence; and
doubly meritorious, conſidering the very
moderate revenue allowed him. We generally

nerally fup there two or three times a week.

This Prince is not often of the King's parties, nor is it imagined that he enjoys a great fhare of his uncle's favour. In what degree he poffeffes the talents of a general is not known, as he was too young to have any command during the late war. But he certainly has a very juft understanding, which has been improved by ftudy. He has taken fome pains to acquire the Englifh language, to which he was induced by an admiration of feveral Englifh authors, whofe works he had read in French and German. He is now able to read Englifh profe with tolerable facility, and has been of late ftudying Shakefpear, having actually read two or three of his plays.

I took the liberty to obferve, that as Shakefpear's genius had traced every labyrinth, and penetrated into every recefs of of the human heart, his fentiments could not fail to pleafe his Royal Highnefs; but, as his language was uncommonly bold and figurative, and full of allufions to national cuftoms, and the manners of our ifland two centuries ago, the Englifh themfelves, who had not made a particular ftudy of his works, did not always comprehend their full energy. I added, that to transfufe the foul of Shakefpear into a tranflation, was impoffible; and to tafte all his beauties in the original, required fuch a knowledge of the Englifh manners and language as few foreigners, even after a long refidence in the capital, could attain.

The Prince faid, he was aware of all this; yet he was determined to ftruggle hard for fome acquaintance with an author fo much admired by the Englifh nation; that though he fhould never be able to tafte all his excellencies, he was convinced he fhould underftand enough to recompence him for his trouble; that he had
already

already ſtudied ſome detached parts, which he thought ſuperior to any thing he had ever met with in the works of any other Poet.

His Royal Highneſs attends to military buſineſs with as much aſſiduity as moſt officers of the ſame rank in the army; for in the Pruſſian ſervice, no degree of eminence in the article of birth can excuſe a remiſſion in the duties of that profeſſion. He is much eſteemed by the army, and conſidered as an exceeding good officer. To the frankneſs of a ſoldier he joins the integrity of a German, and is beloved by the public in general, on account of his good-nature, affability, and humane turn of mind.

LETTER LXXVIII.

Potfdam.

I AM afraid you will think the anecdotes and converfation which I fometimes fend you are rather tedious. Your curiofity about certain characters has led me into this practice; for I choofe to give you opportunities of forming an opinion of your own, rather than to trouble you with mine. My opinion might very probably be erroneous; the accounts I give of what I have feen or heard are always true. And, notwithftanding that the actions and converfations I relate may be apparently of fmall importance, ftill as the perfons in fome meafure defcribe themfelves, an underftanding like yours will be able from thence to draw jufter ideas of character than I could have given.

‡   In

In a former letter I mentioned the great difficulty of deferting from a Pruffian gar- rifon, and of what importance it is thought to prevent it. An accident which happen- ed a few days fince, will give you a ftronger idea of this than any general account.

Two foldiers of the Prince of Pruffia's regiment got over the walls in the night- time, with an intention to defert; but, un- luckily for them, this town ftands on a peninfula formed by the river, and the neck of land is guarded in fuch a manner that it is almoft impoffible to pafs that way without permiffion. Thefe men could not fwim, and they durft not prefent them- felves at any of the ferries, becaufe the boatmen are forbid, under the fevereft penalties, to connive at the efcape of any deferters, and ftriftly ordered to affift in apprehending them. A reward is alfo of- fered, as a greater inducement to this piece of fervice.

All

All thefe circumftances being known in the garrifon, it was imagined that, as none of the peafants would in all probability venture to harbour them, they were ftill fkulking in the fields, among the ftanding corn. On this fuppofition, parties of men were employed for three days fucceffively in traverfing the fields, and beating the bufhcs, as if they had been in chafe of a hare. Great numbers of the officers of this regiment, fome of the higheft rank, rode about for three or four hours every day, all employed in the fame manner. But not finding the men, they were at laft convinced that they had by fome means or other got out of the peninfula, and all further fearch was given up as unneceffary.

On the morning of the fourth day, thefe two unfortunate men came and furrendered to the guard at one of the gates. Finding it impracticable to effect their efcape, and not daring to enter a houfe, they were

at

S

at length compelled, by hunger and fatigue, to deliver themfelves up.

Before I clofe this letter, I will give you an account of an adventure of an affecting nature, which happened in the King's family, at the time when all thefe refearches were made for the two deferters.

The King's principal valet-de-chambre was a man confiderably refpected. Having conftant opportunities of being about the King's perfon, and having enjoyed his approbation for feveral years, people of the firft rank paid him fome degree of attention. He was liked by his acquaintances, as I have been told, on account of his perfonal qualities, and had accumulated a little fortune by the perquifites of his office. He had built a houfe near that of my Lord Marechal, and kept a coach for the ufe of his miftrefs.

It was this man's misfortune to difoblige the King, probably by fome neglect of

duty;

duty; or it might poſſibly be ſomething worſe:—I never could hear exactly how this had happened:—But while the Prin-ceſſes were at the New Palace, the King had blamed him in very ſharp terms; and not being ſatisfied with the excuſes the man made, he told him, that as ſoon as the company was gone, he ſhould be taken care of.

When the Princeſſes went to Berlin, his Majeſty returned to his old palace at Sans-Souci: and the day after, he ſent for an officer of his guards, and ordered him to conduct this man to Potſdam, and place him in the quality of a drummer in the firſt regiment of foot-guards.

The poor man endeavoured to pacify his maſter by prayers and entreaties, but without ſuccefs.—He then ſaid to the of-ficer, that there were ſome things in his room which he wiſhed to put in order be-fore he went, and deſired that he might be

VOL. II.　　　S　　　allowed

allowed a little time for that purpofe. The officer readily affented, and as foon as this defperate man had entered his own apartment, he feized a piftol, which he had prepared from the time the King had threatened him, and immediately fhot himfelf through the head. The report of the piftol alarmed the King and the officer.— They both went into the room, and found the poor creature expiring.

Though the King certainly had no idea that his valet would fhoot himfelf; and though, it is moft probable, he would not have allowed him to remain long in the fituation to which, in a fit of refentment, he had condemned him;—yet there is fomething exceedingly harfh in dafhing a man at once from a fituation of eafe and refpect, into a fphere of life fo very different.—Such an order was more becoming the fury of an intemperate defpot, than the dignity of fo great and fo wife a monarch as the King of Pruffia.

I con-

I converſed with a perſon who had been at Sans-Souci immediately after this me-lancholy event.—He ſaid the King ſeemed to be very much affected.—If he felt it as he ought, he was an object of compaſſion ; if he did not, he was ſtill more ſo, for no-thing can be a greater misfortune to a man than to want humanity.

S 2

LETTER LXXIX.

Drefden.

I Believe I neglected to mention in any of
my letters from Berlin, that when I
vifited the manufactory of porcelain, I was
fo much ftruck with the beauty of fome
of it, that I ordered a fmall box for you.
But as I take it to be a matter of indifference, whether you fip your tea out of the
china you have already, or this, you may
fend it as a prefent to the female you love
and efteem moft. If by this direction it
fhould not go ftraight from you to Mifs
——, pray let me know to whom you fend
it. The factor at Hamburgh will give you
notice when he fhips it off.

I did not imagine that this manufactory
had arrived at fuch a degree of perfection

as

as it has in feveral places in Germany,
particularly at Brunfwic and Berlin. The
parcel I have ordered for you, is thought
equal to the fineft made at Drefden.

The day we left Potfdam we dined with
good Lord Marechal, who took leave of
the Duke, with an emotion which at
once marked his regard for his Grace, and
his fears that he fhould never fee him
again.

If I were ftrongly in a humour for defcription, our journey through the moft
beautiful and moft fertile part of Germany
would afford me a fair opportunity. I not
only could ring over the whole chimes of
woods, meadows, rivers, and mountains,
rich crops of grain, flax, tobacco, and hops;
I might animate the landfcapes with a
copious breed of horfes, black cattle, fheep,
wild boars, and venifon, and vary the defcription with the marble, precious ftones,
and mines of lead, copper, iron, and filver,

S 3   which

which Saxony contains within its bowels.
I might expatiate on the fine china ware,
and fine women, that abound in this country, formed of the fineft clay in Germany,
et très joliment travaillées;—but I am long
fince tired of defcription, and therefore beg
leave to convey you at once from Potfdam
to Drefden.

Having been prefented to the Elector
and Electrefs by Mr. Ofborn, the Britifh
minifter here, we had the honour of dining
with them the fame day. The Electrefs is
young, tall, well-made, and lively.—We
were afterwards prefented to the Electrefs
Dowager, and to the Princefs Elizabeth,
the Elector's aunt, to the Princefs, his
fifter, and to his three brothers, the eldeft
of whom has loft the ufe of his legs, and
is moved about the room in a chair with
wheels.

The court was numerous and fplendid.
in the evening there was card-playing for
about

about two hours.   The Duke of Hamilton was of the Electrefs's party, while I played two rubbers at whift with one of the Princeffes, againft the Electrefs Dowager and the Princefs Elizabeth.—I have never feen deep gaming at any of the German courts.—What has approached neareft to it, has been at mafquerades, or where the Sovereign was not prefent.

Drefden, though not one of the largeft, is certainly one of the moft agreeable cities in Germany, whether we confider its fitu-ation, the magnificence of its palaces, or the beauty and conveniency of the houfes and ftreets.   This city is built on both fides of the Elbe, which is of a confiderable breadth here.   The magnificent and com-modious manner in which the two oppofite parts of the town are joined, adds greatly to its beauty.

There is an equeftrian ftatue of King Auguftus, in a kind of open place or fquare,

between

betwcen the old city and the new. The workmanfhip is but indifferent; however, I was defired by our Cicerone to admire this very much, becaufe——it was made by a common fmith. I begged to be ex-cufed, telling him that I could not admire it, had it been made by Michael Angelo.

Few Princes in Europe are fo magni-ficently lodged as the Elector of Saxony. The Palace and Mufeum have been often defcribed.—The laft was begun by the Elector Auguftus, and ftill retains the name of the Green Room, though it now confifts of feveral apartments, all painted green, in imitation of the firft. I will not enume-rate the prodigious number of curiofities, natural and artificial, to be feen there. Some of the laft are curious, only becaufe they are invifible to the human eye. Of this number, is a cherry ftone, upon which, by the help of a microfcope, above a hundred faces may be diftinguifhed. Undoubtedly thefe little mechanical whims difplay the

labour,

labour, perfeverance, and minute attention of the workman; but I cannot think they are proofs of the wifdom of thofe who could employ artifts to fo little purpofe. Let the aftonifhing minutiæ of nature be admired through microfcopes; but furely nothing is a proper work for the hands of man, which cannot be feen by the unaided human eye.

A work of the jeweller Dinglinger, which reprefents the celebration of the Mogul's birth-day, is much admired. The Mogul fitting on his throne, his grandees and guards, with a great many elephants, are all exhibited upon a table about an ell fquare. This work employed Dinglinger, and fome affiftants, above ten years. Do not you think this was leaving fo ingenious an artift a little too long in the Mogul's fervice?

A fimple lift of every thing valuable and curious in this Mufeum, would exceed
                                            the

the bounds of one of my longeft letters; I fhall therefore pafs them all over in filence, except the ftory of the prophet Jonah, which it would be impious to omit. The fhip, the whale, the prophet, and the fea-fhore, are all reprefented in pearl; but the fea and rocks are in a different kind of ftone, though, in my opinion, there was no occafion to vary the materials: for furely there is as great a difference between a prophet and a whale, as between a whale and a rock. So that if the firft two could be reprefented with the fame materials, I do not think it was worth while to change the compofition for the third.

The gallery of pictures is highly efteemed. To enumerate the particular merits of each, would fill many volumes, and requires a far greater knowledge of painting than I can pretend to. The moft valuable pieces are by Corregio and Rubens. There are three or four by the former, and of his

moft

moſt capital works; and a very conſiderable
number of the latter. The ſtrength and
expreſſion of this great artiſt's pencil, the
natural glow of his colouring, and the fertility of his fancy, deſerve the higheſt encomiums. Yet one cannot help regretting,
that he had ſo violent a paſſion for fat
women. That kind of nature which he
had ſeen early in life in his own country,
had laid ſuch hold of his imagination, that
it could not be eradicated by all the elegant models he afterwards ſtudied in
Italy. Some of his female figures in
this gallery are ſo much of the Dutch
make, and ſo fat, that it is rather op-
preſſive to look at them in this very hot
weather.

In the Muſeum, within the Palace, there
is a moſt complete collection of prints, from
the commencement of the art of engraving
till the preſent time.

LETTER LXXX.

Drefden.

NOTHING feems clearer to me, than that a fortified town fhould have no palaces within it, and no fuburbs without. As the city of Drefden has both, it would have been well for the inhabitants, during the laft war, that the town had been entirely without fortifications. In the year 1756, when the King of Pruffia thought it expedient to invade Saxony, he made himfelf mafter of this city, and kept peaceable poffeffion of it till 1758, when Marechal Daun, after the battle of Hochkirchen, threatened to befiege it. The Pruffian General Schmettau began his defence by burning part of the fuburbs. The Saxons and Auftrians exclaimed at this meafure, and Daun threatened to

make

make the governor anfwerable, in his own perfon, for fuch defperate proceedings. Count Schmettau was totally regardlefs of their exclamations and threats, and feemed attentive only to the orders of the King his mafter. He gave Marechal Daun to underftand, that the remaining fuburbs would fhare the fate of thofe already deftroyed, if he perfifted in attacking the town. The King appearing foon after, the Auftrians retreated into Bohemia.

The inhabitants of Drefden, and all Saxony, were now in a very difmal fituation, and found their hardfhips increafe in proportion to the fuccefs of their friends and allies; for whatever exactions were raifed in the King of Pruffia's dominions by the Auftrians and Ruffians, the like were impofed by way of retaliation on the miferable Saxons. A people muft be in a deplorable ftate indeed, when the fuccefs of their enemies is the moft fortunate thing which can befal them.

In

In 1759, after the dreadful battle of Cunerſdorf, near Frankfort on the Oder, the King of Pruſſia being neceſſitated to repair the ſlaughter of that day, withdrew the Pruſſian garriſon from Dreſden, which then fell into the hands of the Imperialiſts. But the calamities of this city did not end here; for his Pruſſian Majeſty having deceived Marechal Daun by a very maſterly feint, while he ſeemed to bend his courſe for Sileſia, he wheeled ſuddenly about, and threatened Dreſden, which Marechal Daun had abandoned, in the full conviction, that the King had marched to the relief of Schweidnitz. While the Auſtrians hurried on by forced marches into Sileſia, the King attacked Dreſden, which was reſolutely defended by General Macquire.

Every poſſible effort was made to reduce this city before Count Daun ſhould return to its relief;—and the wretched citizens

were

were expofed to a continued cannonade and
bombardment. This perhaps was jufti-
fiable by the laws of war, as long as there
were hopes that the town might be
brought to furrender by fuch means.——
But the enemies of his Pruffian Majefty
affert, that the bombardment was continued, and churches, fine buildings, and
whole ftreets, laid in afhes, even after
Marechal Daun's return; and when thefe
vindictive proceedings could only tend to
the ruin and deftruction of private people,
without contributing in the fmalleft degree to the reducing the town, or being of
any ufe to the public caufe.

Many of thefe houfes ftill lie in rub-
bifh; but the inhabitants are gradually
rebuilding, and probably all the ruined
ftreets will be repaired before a new war
breaks out in Germany. While they re-
build the houfes, I cannot help thinking
it would be fortunate for the proprietors,
that

that they were allowed to deftroy the fortifications, which perhaps might be placed
with more advantage around fome towns
on the frontiers.

The curious manufactory of porcelain
fuffered confiderably by the Pruffian bombardment. The Elector has a complete
collection of the fineft pieces, from the
firft attempts made here in this elegant
work, to the lateft improvements. This,
independent of the beauty of many of the
pieces, is a matter of real curiofity, as
it marks the progrefs of ingenuity and invention.

Our morning-walk is in the gardens of
the late Count Bruhl, fituated on the high
banks of the Elbe. Nothing can be imagined more delightful than the view from
a lofty terrace in thefe gardens. The
Count's magnificent houfe is now ftript
of many of its greateft ornaments. The
fine collection of paintings has been fold
to the Emprefs of Ruffia for 150,000 rix-
dollars.

dollars.³ The library, which is in the garden, is two hundred and twenty feet long.
I am not certain, whether it was abfolutely neceffary to have fo large a room
for containing this nobleman's books; but
it muft have required one of that fize at
leaft for his wardrobe, if the account that
is given of it be juft. They tell us, that
the Count had at leaft three hundred different fuits of clothes; each of thefe had a
duplicate, as he always fhifted his clothes
after dinner, and did not choofe that his
drefs fhould appear different in the afternoon from what it had been in the morning. A painting of each fuit, with the
particular cane and fnuff-box belonging to
it, was very accurately drawn in a large
book, which was prefented to his Excellency every morning by his Valet de Cham-
bre, that he might fix upon the drefs in
which he wifhed to appear for the day.
This minifter was accufed of having accu-

mulated a great fortune. The reverſe
of this, however, is true. His houſe and
gardens belong now to the Elector.

The Saxon troops make a very fine appearance. The men in general are handſome and well made. Neither they nor
their officers' are ſo very upright and ſtiff
in their manners, as the Pruſſians. Having been ſo long accuſtomed to theſe laſt,
this difference ſtruck me very ſtrongly at
firſt ſight. The uniform of the guards is
red and yellow; that of the marching regiments white. The ſoldiers, during the
ſummer, wear only waiſtcoats, even when
they mount guard; and always appear
extremely neat and clean. The ſerjeants,
beſides their other arms, have a large piſtol.
This is ſo commodiouſly faſtened to the
left ſide, that it gives no trouble. The
band of muſic belonging to the Saxon
guards is the moſt complete and the fineſt
I ever ſaw.

4

I do

I do not expect to receive any accounts from you till we arrive at Vienna; but I shall probably write again from Prague, for which place we intend to set out to-morrow.

T 2

LETTER LXXXI.

Prague.

BOHEMIA, though by no means so fertile, or so fine a country as Saxony, does not deserve the bad character which some travellers have given it. I thought many places very beautiful, and varied with the most agreeable rural objects.

Prague, the capital of Bohemia, stands in a hollow, surrounded on all sides with hills. Those nearest the town, and which command it, are comprehended within the fortifications. It is a very large town, retaining some marks of former splendor, but many more evident symptoms of present decay—Symptoms which naturally attend those places which once have been the residence of royalty, and are so no more.

All

All the houfes, with any appearance of magnificence, are old, and it is not probable that any new ones will be built in that ftyle: for the Bohemian nobility, who are in circumftances to bear fuch an expence, live at Vienna, and the trade and manufactures of this town are not fufficient to enable any of the mercantile people to build fine houfes.

In whatever degree this city may have dwindled in wealth and magnificence, the piety of the inhabitants certainly flourifhes as much as ever. I do not recollect to have feen fo many glaring marks of devotion in any place. The corners of the ftreets, bridges, and public buildings, are all ornamented with crucifixes, images of the Virgin of all fizes and complexions, and ftatues of Saints of every country, condition, age, and fex. People are to be feen on their knees before thefe ftatues in every part of this city, but particularly on the large bridge over the Moldaw, where

T 3

there

there is the greateſt concourſe of paſſen-
gers. This bridge is ſo profuſely adorned
with the ſtatues of Saints, that, croſſing over
it, you have a row of them on each ſide,
like two ranks of muſketeers.

Travellers, eſpecially ſuch as arrive directly from Berlin, muſt be aſtoniſhed at
the people's devotion in this city, and in a
particular manner at the vehemence with
which it is expreſſed by thoſe who exhibit
before the Saints upon the bridge.

Not contented with kneeling, I ſaw ſome
proſtrate themſelves on their faces, kiſſing
the earth ; and others, who offered their
petitions to theſe Saints with ſuch earneſt-
neſs and fervour, that, if their hearts had
not been of ſtone, they muſt have paid
more attention to the petitioners than they
ſeemed to do.

There is one ſaint who has more votaries
than all the reſt put together—Saint Nepomuc, I think they call him :—As my
acquaint-

acquaintance with Saints is not extenfive, I never heard of him till I came hither, but his reputation is very great in this town. This faint, it feems, was ordered by fome cruel tyrant, to be thrown over a bridge, his neck was broke by the fall, notwithftanding of which, he is fuppofed to retain a particular affection for bridges ever fince; an effect fomething different from what was to have been expected from the caufe; however, the people here are perfuaded, that fo it happened to Saint Nepomuc; and to put the fact beyond controverfy, he is at this moment the tutelar Saint of bridges;—almoft all thofe in Bohemia are dedicated to him. He has alfo the reputation of excelling every Saint in heaven in the cure of barrennefs in women. —How his character for this was eftablifhed, I did not enquire.

It is a melancholy reflection, that the wealthy are more carelefs about religious duties than the indigent, and that poverty

and

and piety are fo often linked together. I often obferved, when we ftopped at any town or village, which had fymptoms of great poverty, that the inhabitants feemed alfo unufually devout.

It would appear, that hope is a more powerful fentiment in the human breaft than gratitude, fince thofe who ought to feel the greateft thankfulnefs to Heaven, difplay the leaft.

We found an acquaintance at Prague when we leaft expected it; for as the Duke of Hamilton and I ftood talking in the ftreets, a prieft, who belongs to a feminary of learning in this town, overheard us; up-on which he ftopped, and after looking at us very earneftly for fome time, he at length came up, and addreffed us in thefe words:—I do affure you now, I am an Irifhman too. This eafy kind of introduc-tion foon produced a degree of intimacy; I afked, how he knew fo readily that we were Irifh? Am I not after hearing you

fpeak

fpeak Englifh, my dear? replied the honeft prieft, for he really was a very honeft obliging fellow, and the moft ufeful and entertaining Cicerone we could have had at Prague.

After having vifited the royal apartments, they fhewed us the window in the fecretary of ftate's office, from whence three noblemen were thrown in the year 1618. This was rather a violent mode of turning out the people in power; but it is probable the party in oppofition had tried gentler means in vain.

As one great ufe of hiftory is to furnifh leffons and examples, by which pofterity in all ages may profit, I do not think it would be amifs to remind your friends in adminiftration of this adventure, that they may move off quietly before their opponents take defperate meafures. For it has been obferved, that the enemies of tottering ftatefmen are much more active than
their

their friends, who when things come to
the laſt puſh, are apt to ſtand aloof,

> Like people viewing, at a diſtance,
> Three men thrown out of a caſement,
> Who never ſtir to their aſſiſtance,
> But juſt afford them their amazement.

In caſe however a ſimilar outrage ſhould be
threatened in England, it is to be hoped
that Apollo (as he was wont of old when
any of his friends were in danger) will in-
terpoſe with a cloud, and ſave the Mi-
niſter; for, in the preſent ſcarcity of wit
and good-humour, it would be a thouſand
pities to loſe a man ſo much diſtinguiſhed
for both, at one deſperate throw.

We walked over the heights, from which
the Pruſſians attempted to carry the town,
immediately after the defeat of Prince
Charles of Lorraine and Count Brown.
The bombardment of this town was a
more defenſible meaſure than that of Dreſden; for while the army within were
under

under the dejection natural after the lofs of a battle, and unprepared for a fiege, it might be fuppofed, that the confufion and terror produced by the bombardment, joined to the vaft confumption of provifions by fuch a numerous garrifon, would induce the befieged to furrender. But although the King's humanity has not been called in queftion for his conduct here, I have heard many military men cenfure him for want of prudence, particularly on account of his defperate attempt at Kolin, when, leaving the half of his army to continue the blockade of Prague, he marched with little more than thirty thoufand men, and attacked an army of double that number, ftrongly fituated, and commanded by one of the ableft generals of the age.

After all, it is more than probable, that the King had very good reafons for his conduct. But as the attempt was unfuccefsful, and as the fad reverfe of the Pruffian affairs may be dated from that epoch, the

voice

voice of cenfure has been very loud in blaming an action, which would have been exalted to the fkies had it been crowned with fuccefs. If Hannibal had by any accident been defeated at Cannæ, it is very poffible, that hiftorians would have found out many reafons why he fhould not have fought that battle, and would have endeavoured to prove, that his former victories had been gained by chance, and that he was a mere ignoramus in the art of war.

Adieu, my good friend; I wifh you good luck in all your undertakings, that you may continue to be reckoned by the world, a man of prudence.

LETTER LXXXII.

Vienna.

ON arriving at Vienna, the poſtillions drive directly to the Cuſtom-houſe, where the baggage undergoes a very ſevere ſcrutiny, which neither fair words nor money can mitigate. As nothing contraband was found among our baggage, it was all carried directly to our lodgings, except our books, which were retained to be examined at leiſure, and were not reſtored to us till ſome time after. The Empreſs has given ſtrict orders, that no books of impiety, lewdneſs, or immorality, ſhall be allowed to enter her dominions, or be circulated among her ſubjects; and Mahomet himſelf dares as ſoon appear publicly at Vienna as any one of them.

Unfortu-

Unfortunately for us, Sir Robert Keith is lately gone to England, and is not expected back for several months. We have reason to regret the abfence of fo agreeable and fo worthy a man; but every advantage we could have received from him as a minifter, has been fupplied by his fecretary, Mr. Erneft; who has introduced us to the Count Degenfeldt, ambaffador from the States-General. This gentleman furnifhed us with a lift of the vifits proper to be made, and had the politenefs to attend the Duke of Hamilton on this grand tour.

The firft day we waited on Prince Kaunitz, we were invited to dine, and found a very numerous company at his houfe; many of whom, as I afterwards underftood, had been prepoffeffed in our favour, by the polite and obliging letters which the Baron de Swieten had written from Berlin.

Some of the principal families are at their feats in the country, which we fhould have more reafon to regret, were it not

for

for the politenefs and hofpitality of the
Count and Countefs Thune, at whofe houfe,
or that of their fifter the Countefs Walftein,
there is an agreeable party every evening;
among whom is the Vifcount de Laval,
brother to the Marquis, whom I had the
honour of knowing at Berlin. The Vifcount has been as far north as Peterfburg,
and intends to make the tour of Italy before
he returns to France.

The city of Vienna, properly fo called,
is not of very great extent; nor can it be
enlarged, being limited by a ftrong fortifi-
cation. This town is very populous: it is
thought to contain above feventy thoufand
inhabitants. The ftreets in general are
narrow, and the houfes built high. Some
of the public buildings and palaces are
magnificent; but they appear externally to
no great advantage, on account of the nar-
rownefs of the ftreets. The chief are the
Imperial Palace, the Library and Mufeum,
the palaces of the Princes Lichtenftein,
Eugene,

Eugene, and fome others, which I know you will excufe me from enumerating or defcribing.

There is no great danger that Vienna will ever again be fubjected to the inconveniencies of a fiege. Yet, in cafe the thing fhould happen, a meafure has been taken, which will prevent the neceffity of deftroying the fuburbs: No houfes without the walls are allowed to be built nearer to the glacis than fix hundred yards; fo that there is a circular field of fix hundred paces broad all round the town, which, exclufive of the advantage above mentioned, has a very beautiful and falutary effect. Beyond the plain, the fuburbs are built.—They form a very extenfive and magnificent town, of an irregularly circular form, containing within its bofom a fpacious field, which has for its centre the original town of Vienna.

Thefe magnificent fuburbs, and the town together, are faid to contain above three

hundred

hundred thoufand inhabitants; yet the former are not near fo populous, in proportion to their fize, as the town; becaufe many houfes of the fuburbs have extenfive gardens belonging to them, and many families, who live during the winter within the fortifications, pafs the fummer months in the fuburbs.

Monfieur de Breteuil, the French ambaffador, lives there at prefent. The Duke and I dined at his houfe a few days ago. This gentleman was attached to the Duc de Choifeul, and had been appointed ambaffador to this court, in which character he was about to fet out from Paris, when that minifter was difmiffed by the late King of France; upon which M. de Breteuil inftead of Vienna, was fent to Naples. But fince the new King's acceffion, he has been eftablifhed at the court for which he was originally intended. He is a man of talents, and not calculated for a fituation in which talents have little or no room for exertion.

About a week after our arrival at Vienna, we had the honour of being prefented to the Emperor. The Count Degenfeldt accompanied us to the palace between nine and ten in the morning. After walking a few minutes in an adjoining room, we were conducted into that where the emperor was alone. His manner is affable, cafy, and gracefully plain.

The fame forenoon we drove to Schohbrun, a palace about a league from Vienna, where the Emprefs refides at prefent. I had no fmall curiofity to fee the celebrated Maria Therefa, whofe fortunes have interefted Europe for fo many years. Her magnanimity in fuppotting the calamities to which the early part of her life was expofed, and the moderation with which fhe has borne profperity, have fecured to her univerfal approbation. She alfo was alone when we were prefented.

prefented. She converfed for fome time with the Duke of Hamilton in an eafy and cheerful manner, and behaved to all with an affable dignity. She now poffeffes but fmall remains of that beauty for which fhe was diftinguifhed in her youth; but her countenance indicates benevolence and good-humour. I had often heard of the fcrupulous etiquette of the Imperial court, but have found every thing directly oppofite to that account.

Prince Kaunitz having feen a young Englifh gentleman fcarcely fourteen years of age, whom the Duke of Hamilton patronizes, and who has accompanied us on this tour, the Prince defired that he alfo might be prefented to the Emperor and Emprefs, which was accordingly done, and they both received him in the moft gracious manner. I mention this circumftance as a ftrong proof how far they are fuperior at this court to trifling punctilios, and how greatly

U 2   they

they have relaxed in ceremony since the accession of the Lorrain family.

Two or three days after this, we were presented at a full court, to the two unmarried Arch-duchesses, their sister the Princess Albert of Saxony, and the Princess of Modena, who is married to the Emperor's brother. The last couple are lately arrived from Milan on a visit to the Empress.

The Imperial family are uncommonly well-looking, and have a very strong resemblance to each other. They are all of a fair complexion, with large blue eyes, and some of them, particularly the Arch-duke, are distinguished by the thick lip so long remarked in the Austrian family. The beautiful Queen of France is the handsomest of this family, only because she is the youngest; some people think that her sister the Princess Albert has still the advantage.

One

One of the unmarried Arch-ducheſſes, who formerly was thought the moſt beautiful, has ſuffered conſiderably by the ſmall-pox.—A lady of the court told me, that, as ſoon as this princeſs underſtood what her diſeaſe was, ſhe called for a looking-glaſs, and with unaffected pleaſantry took leave of thoſe features ſhe had often heard praiſed, and which ſhe believed would be greatly changed before ſhe ſhould ſee them again. The diminution which the ſmall-pox has made in the beauty of this Princeſs, has not in the ſmalleſt degree impaired her good-humour, or the eſſential part of her character, which by every account is perfectly amiable.

When the King of Pruſſia ſaw his army defeated at Cunerſdorf, after he had written to the Queen that he was ſure of victory; or when any of thoſe monarchs, of whom hiſtory gives examples, were daſhed from their thrones to a ſtate of dependence or captivity, unqueſtionably it required great

U 3   ſtrength

ſtrength of mind to bear ſuch cruel reverſes of fortune ; but perhaps it requires more in a woman, whoſe beauty is admired by one half of the human race, and envied by the other, to ſupport its loſs with equanimity in all the pride of youth.—If thoſe veteran beauties, who never had any thing but their faces to give them importance, whom we ſee ſtill withering on the ſtalk, and repining that they cannot retain the bloom of May in the froſt of December, had met with ſuch an accident, it would probably have killed them at once, and ſaved them many years of deſpiſed exiſtence.

LETTER LXXXIII.

Vienna.

I Never paffed my time more agreeably than fince I came to Vienna. There is not fuch a conftant round of amufements as to fill up a man's time without any plan or occupation of his own; and yet there is enough to fatisfy any mind not perfectly vacant and dependent on external objects.—— We dine abroad two or three times a week. We fometimes fee a little play, but never any deep gaming.——At the Countefs Thune's, where I generally pafs the evening, there is no play of any kind.—The fociety there literally form a converfazione.

I dare fay, you will be at a lofs to imagine how a mixed company, fometimes pretty numerous, can pafs feveral hours every

U 4 evening,

evening, merely in converfing, efpecially when you are told that the converfation is not always fplit into parties and tête-à-têtes; but is very often general. You will fufpect there muft be many melancholy paufes, which, after a certain length, are prolonged, from the reluctance of people to be the firft breakers of a very folemn filence; or you may think that fometimes there will be fo many tongues moving at once, that nothing can be heard diftinctly; and you may poffibly figure to yourfelf the lady of the houfe at other times endeavouring, by formal obfervations on the weather, or politics, to keep alive a converfation which is juft expiring in all the yawnings of death.

Nothing of this kind, however, happens. The Countefs has the art of entertaining a company, and of making them entertain one another, more than any perfon I ever knew. With a great deal of wit, and a perfect knowledge of the world, fhe poffeffes the moft difinterefted heart. She is the firft to difcover

difcover the good qualities of her friends,
and the laft who fees their foibles. One of
her greateft pleafures is to remove prejudices from amongft her acquaintances, and
to promote friendfhips. She has an ever-
lafting flow of fpirits, which fhe manages
with fuch addrefs as to delight the gay, without difpleafing the dejected. I never knew
any body have fuch a number of friends,
and fo much generous friendfhip to beftow
on each : She is daily making new ones,
without allowing her regard for the old to
diminifh. She has formed a little fyftem of
happinefs at her own houfe, herfelf being
the centre of attraction and union. Nobody
is under the leaft neceffity of remaining a
moment in this fociety after being tired.—
They may retire when they pleafe.—No
more notice is taken of the entries or exits
of any perfon who has been once received,
than of a fly's coming in or going out of
the room.—There is not the fhadow of reftraint.—If you go every night, you are
always

always treated with equal kindnefs; and if you ftay away for a month, you are received on your return with the fame cheerfulnefs as if you had been there every evening.

The Englifh who come to this place are in a particular manner obliged to this family, not only for the polite reception they generally meet with, but alfo for the opportunities this affords them of forming an acquaintance with the principal people at Vienna. And I imagine there is no city in Europe where a young gentleman, after his univerfity education is finifhed, can pafs a year with fo great advantage; becaufe, if properly recommended, he may mix, on an eafy footing, with people of rank, and have opportunities of improving by the converfation of fenfible men and accomplifhed women. In no capital could he fee fewer examples, or have fewer opportunities of deep gaming, open profligacy, or grofs debauchery. He may learn to pafs his time agreeably, independent of a continued round
of

of amufements.—He may be gradually led to enjoy rational converfation, and at length acquire the blcffed faculty of being fatisfied with moderate pleafures.

To the politenefs of the Countefs Thune, and the recommendation of the Baron Swieten, I am indebted for the agreeable footing I am on with Prince Kaunitz, who at prefent lives at Laxenberg, a pleafant village about ten miles from Vienna, where there is a fmall palace and very extenfive park, belonging to the Imperial family.

Prince Kaunitz has lately built a houfe there, and lives in a ftyle equally hofpitable and magnificent. He is not to be feen before dinner by any but people on bufinefs; but he always has a pretty large company at dinner, and ftill greater numbers from Vienna pafs their evenings at Laxenberg; not unfrequently the Emperor himfelf makes one of the company. This minifter has enjoyed the favour of the Emprefs for many years.

years. He was her envoy at the treaty of
Aix-la-Chapelle in 1748, and has been of
her cabinet council ever fince. At prefent
he is minifter for all foreign affairs, and is
fuppofed to have greater influence with her
than any other perfon.

He is certainly a man of knowledge,
genius, and fidelity, and the affairs of this
court have profpered greatly under his management. His friends are very much attached to him, and he fhews great difcernment in difcovering, and employing men of
talents. He is the friend and patron of
Monf. de Swieten. It is fuppofed that he
advifed and negociated the French alliance,
yet he has always had a ftrong partiality in
favour of the Britifh nation.—He has fome
fingularities; but as they do not affect any
effential part of his character, they need not
be mentioned.

LETTER LXXXIV.

Vienna.

I Had the pleafure of yours by the laft poft, wherein you inform me that our acquaintance C—— talks of fetting out for Vienna very foon. As nothing is fo tirefome as the company of one who is continually tired of himfelf, I fhould be alarmed at your information, were I not abfolutely certain that his ftay here will be very fhort, come when he will.

C— called at my lodgings one morning the fummer before I had left London.—I had remained in town merely becaufe I had no particular bufinefs elfewhere;—but he affured me, that the town was a defert;— that it was fhameful to be feen in the ftreets;—that all the world was at Brighthelmftone.—

helmftone.—So I allowed him to conduct
me to that place, where we had remained
only a few days, when he told me, that
none of the people he cared for were there;
and as I had nothing particular to detain
me, he begged as a favour that I would accompany him to Tunbridge.—We went
accordingly, and to my great fatisfaction
I there found Mr. N——'s family. C——
remained pretty quiet for about four days;
—he yawned a good deal on the fifth;—
and on the fixth, I thought he would have
diflocated his jaws. As he perceived I was
pleafed with the place, and would take none
of his hints about leaving it, he at laft pretended that he had received a letter which
made it abfolutely neceffary for him to fet
out for London:—and away he went.

I ftaid three weeks at Tunbridge.—On
my return to town, I underftood that C——
had taken a genteel furnifhed houfe for the
fummer in Yorkfhire, where he had already
paffed a week, having previoufly engaged a
                                        female

female friend to go along with him.—He
left word in town, that he was not to be
expected till the meeting of parliament.
Though I never imagined that he would
remain quite fo long, yet I was a little furprifed to fee him enter my room two days
after I had received this account.—He told
me, he was quite difgufted with his houfe,
and more fo with his companion:—and befides, he had taken a violent fancy to go to
Paris, which you know, added he, is the
moft delightful place in the world, efpecially
in fummer; for the company never think
of rambling about the country like our
giddy fools in England, but remain together in the capital as fenfible people ought
to do.

He then propofed that we fhould pack
up a few things,—take poft,—pafs over,—
and fpend a couple of months at Paris.
Finding I did not relifh the propofal, he
wrote an apology to the lady in Yorkfhire,
with an inclofed bank bill, and fet out next

8   day

day by himſelf. I heard no more of him for ſix weeks, but at the end of that time happening to be at Bath, I ſaw my friend C— enter the pump-room.—'Egad, ſaid he, you were wiſe to ſtay at home:—Paris is become the moſt inſipid place on earth :—I could not ſupport it above ten days.—But having heard a good deal of Holland, I even took a jaunt to Amſterdam, which, between friends, I found very little more amuſing than Paris; two days after my arrival, finding an Engliſh ſhip juſt ready to ſail, I thought it would be a pity to let the opportunity ſlip. So I ordered my trunk aboard. —We had a diſagreeable paſſage:—However, I arrived ſafe a few days ago at Harwich. After this ſketch of poor C—'s turn of mind, you ſee, I have no reaſon to fear his remaining long with us, if he ſhould come.

Foreigners aſſert that the Engliſh have more of this reſtleſs diſpoſition than any other people in Europe.

Il faut que votre ville de Londres foit un trifte féjour.—I afked the perfon who made this remark to me, wherefore he thought fo? —Parceque, anfwered he, tous vos jeunes gens que je vois en France s'ennuyent à la mort.—But, faid I, there are a great many of your countrymen in London.—Affurément, anfwered he, with polite infolence, cela fait une différence.

Our climate is accufed of producing this ennuy. If I rightly remember, I formerly hinted fome reafons againft this opinion, and of late I begin to fufpect that the exceffive wealth of certain individuals, and the ftate of fociety in our capital, are the fole caufes of our having a greater fhare of that malady among us than our neighbours. The common people of England know nothing of it:—neither do the induftrious of any rank, whether their object be wealth, knowledge, or fame. But in England there is a greater number than in any other country, of young men, who come to the poffeffion of great fortunes before they have acquired any fixed and determined tafte, which may ferve as a refource and occupation through life.

When a youth has acquired a habit of application, a thirft of knowledge, or of fame, the moft ample fortune which can fall to him afterwards, cannot always deftroy difpofitions and paffions already formed—Particularly if the paffion be ambition, which generally gives fuch energy to the mind, and occafions fuch continued exertions as fufficiently ward off laffitude and tædium ; for wealth cannot lull, or pleafure enervate, a mind ftrongly infpired by that active principle. Such therefore are out of the prefent queftion. But when a full and uncontrolled command of money comes firft, and every object of pleafure is placed within the reach of the unambitious, all other purfuits are too frequently defpifed ; and every tafte or accomplifhment which could inform or

ftrengthen

ſtrengthen the mind, and fill up the tedious
intervals of life, is neglected.

A young man in this ſituation is prone to
excefs ; he ſeldom waits the natural returns
of appetite of any kind ;—his ſenſibility is
blunted by too frequent enjoyment ;—what
is deſired to-day, is lothed to-morrow ;—
every thing at a diſtance, which bears the
name of pleaſure, is an object of deſire ;—
when preſent, it becomes an object of indifference, if not of diſguſt.—The agitations
of gaming are tried to prevent the horrid
ſtagnation of indolence :—All amuſements
loſe their reliſh, and ſerve to increaſe the
langour they were meant to expel.

As age advances, caprice, peeviſhneſs,
and tædium augment :—The ſcene is often
changed ; but the ſame fretful piece is conſtantly acted till the curtain is dropt, or
is pulled down by the impatient actor himſelf before the natural end of the drama.

X 2   Does

Does not all this happen in France and Germany?—Doubtlefs; but not fo often as in England, for the reafons already mentioned. In France, a very fmall proportion of young men have the uncontrolled poffeffion of great fortunes. They have not the means of gratifying every defire, and indulging every caprice. Inftead of fpending their time in clubs or taverns with people of their own age, the greater part of the young nobility pafs their evenings with fome private family, or in thofe focieties of both fexes to which they have the entrée. There the decorum due to fuch company reftrains, of courfe, the vivacity and wantonnefs of their behaviour and converfation; and adventures occur which intereft and amufe, without being followed by the naufea, languor, and remorfe, which often fucceed nights fpent at the gaming-table, or the licentioufnefs of tavern fuppers.

Nothing has a better influence on the temper, difpofition, and manners of a young perfon,

perfon, than living much in the company of thofe whom he refpeéts. Exclufive of the improvement he may receive from their converfation, he is habituated to felf-denial, and muft relinquifh many indulgences which lead to indolence and languor.

The young French nobility, even although they fhould have no great fhare of ambition, no love of ftudy, no particular turn for any of thofe higher accomplifhments which enable men to pafs the hours of life independent of other amufements; yet they contrive to keep tædium at a diftance by efforts of a different kind, by a fpecies of aétivity peculiar to themfelves: They perceive, very early in life, the abfolute neceffity of pleafing; this fentiment pervades their general conduét, and goes a great way in the formation of their real charaéter. They are attentive and obliging to all, and particularly endeavour to acquire and retain the friendfhip of thofe who can affift their fortunes; and they have a relifh for life,

becaufe

becaufe it is not always in their power to anticipate enjoyment, nor can they cloy their appetites by fatiety. Even the moft diffipated among them are unacquainted with the unbounded freedom of a tavern life, where all the freaks of a whimfical mind, and a capricious tafte, may be indulged without hefitation, and which, after long indulgence, renders every other kind of fociety infupportable.

With regard to the Germans, there are very few men of great independent fortunes among them. The little princes, by whom the riches of the country are engroffed, have, I fufpect, their own difficulties to get through life with any tolerable degree of fatisfaction. As for their younger brothers and the middling gentry, they go into the army, and are fubjected to the rigorous and unremitting attentions of military difcipline. This, of confequence, forms a character, in many refpects different from that of the Englifh or French gentleman,

But

But I have not yet mentioned the circumftance, which, of all others, perhaps
contributes the moft to render London the
trifte féjour which foreigners often find it;
I mean the eftablifhment of clubs, from
which that part of the community are excluded who have the greateft power to
foothe the cares, and enliven the pleafures
of life.

LETTER LXXXV.

Vienna.

WE had an invitation lately from Monf. de Breteuil to dine on the top of Mount Calenberg, a very high mountain in the neighbourhood of this city. Common coaches or chariots cannot be dragged up; but having driven to the bottom, we found chaifes of a particular conftruction, calculated for fuch expeditions. Thefe had been ordered by the Ambaffador for the accommodation of the company, and in them we were carried to the fummit, where there is a convent of Monks, from which two landfcapes of very oppofite natures appear. The one confifts of a feries of wild mountains; the other, of the town, fuburbs, and environs of Vienna, with the various

branches

branches of the Danube flowing through a rich champaign of boundlefs extent.

The table for dinner was covered in a field near the convent, under the fhade of fome trees.--Every delicacy of the feafon was ferved up.——Madame de Matignon, a very beautiful and fprightly lady, daughter of M. de Breteuil, did the honours.—— Some of the fineft women of Vienna, her companions, were of the company; and the whole entertainment was conducted with equal tafte and gaiety.

During the deffert, fome of the Fathers came and prefented the company with bafkets of fruit and fallad from their garden.—The Ambaffador invited them to fit, and the ladies pledged them in tokay. Monf. de Breteuil had previoufly obtained permiffion for the ladies to enter the convent;——which they accordingly did, as foon as they rofe from table, attended by all the company.

You

You will readily believe, that the appearance of fo many handfome women would be particularly interefting to a community which had never before beheld a female within their walls.—This indeed was fufficiently evident, in fpite of the gravity and mortified looks of the Fathers.

One lady of a gay difpofition laid hold of a little fcourge which hung at one of the Fathers' belts, and defired he would make her a prefent of it, for fhe wifhed to ufe it when fhe returned home, having, as fhe faid, been a great finner.——The Father, with great gallantry, begged fhe would fpare her own fair fkin, affuring her that he would give himfelf a hearty flogging on her account that very evening;— and to prove how much he was in earneft, fell directly on his knees before a little altar, and began to whip his own fhoulders with great earneftnefs, declaring, that when the ladies fhould retire, he would lay it

with

with the fame violence on his naked body; for he was determined fhe fhould be as free from fin as fhe was on the day of her birth.

This melted the heart of the lady.—She begged the Father might take no more of her faults upon his fhoulders.———She now affured him that her flips had been very venial, and that fhe was convinced what he had already done would clear her as completely as if he fhould whip himfelf to the bone.

There is fomething fo ludicrous in all this, that you may naturally fufpect the reprefentation I have given, proceeds from invention rather than memory. I affure you, however, in downright earneft, that the fcene paffed nearly as defcribed; and, to prevent farther mifchief, I put the fcourge, which the zealous Father had made ufe of, in my pocket.

On

On my return to Vienna, I called the
fame evening at the Countefs Walftein's,
and foon after the Emperor came there.
Somebody had already mentioned to him
the pious gallantry of the Father at the top
'of Mount Calenberg.—He afked for a fight
of the whip, which he underftood I had
brought away:—I had it ftill in my pocket,
and immediately fhowed it him.——He
laughed very heartily at the warmth of the
Father's zeal, which he fuppofed had been
augmented by the Ambaffador's tokay.

You have often heard of the unceremo-
nious and eafy manner in which this great
Prince lives with his fubjects. Report cannot exaggerate on this head. The Countefs
Walftein had no expectations of his vifiting
her that evening.——When the fervant
named the Emperor before he entered, I
ftarted up, and was going to retire.—The
Countefs defired me to remain, for nothing
was more difagreeable to him than that any
company fhould be difturbed on his entering.—

ing.—The ladies kept their feats, fome of them knotting all the time he remained. The men continued ftanding while he ftood, and when he was feated, moft part of them fat down alfo.—The Emperor put Count Mahoni, the Spanifh ambaffador, in mind of his gout, and made him fit while him-felf remained ftanding.

This monarch converfes with all the eafe and affability of a private gentleman, and gradually feduces others to talk with the fame eafe to him.   He is furely much hap-pier in this noble condefcenfion, and muft acquire a more perfect knowledge of man-kind, than if he kept himfelf aloof from his fubjects, continually wrapt up in his own importance and the Imperial fur.

LETTER LXXXVI.

Vienna.

THE manners of this court are confiderably altered fince Lady Mary Wortley Montague was here, particularly fince the acceffion of the prefent Emprefs, whofe underftanding and affability have abridged many of the irkfome ceremonials formerly in ufe. Her fon's philofophical turn of mind, and the amiable and conciliating characters of her whole family, have no doubt tended to put fociety in general upon a more eafy and agreeable footing.

People of different ranks now do bufinefs together with eafe, and meet at public places without any of thofe ridiculous difputes about precedency, of which the ingenious Englifh lady has given fuch lively defcriptions.

defcriptions.—Yet trifling punctilios are not fo completely banifhed, as, I imagine, the Emperor could wifh, he himfelf being the leaft punctilious perfon in his dominions:— for there is certainly ftill a greater feparation than good fenfe would direct, between the various claffes of the fubjects.—The fentiments of a people change very gradually, and it takes a courfe of years before reafon, or even the example of the Sovereign, can overcome old cuftoms and prejudices.

The higher, or ancient families, keep themfelves as diftinct from the inferior, or newly-created nobility, as thefe do from the citizens: So that it is very difficult for the inferior claffes to be in fociety, or to have their families much 'connected with thofe of the fuperior ranks. And, what is of more importance in a political fenfe, there are certain places of high truft in the government, which cannot be occupied by any but the higher order of nobility.

Would

Would you not think it difadvantageous for a government to keep a law in force which enacts, that the offices in the ftate which require the greateft abilities, fhould be filled from that clafs of the community in which there is the leaft chance of finding them?—Perhaps the ufage above mentioned is nearly equivalent to fuch a law. As for the peafants, who are entirely out of the queftion, they are, in many parts of the Emperor's dominions, in a ftate of perfect flavery, and almoft totally dependant on the proprietors of the land.

The ideas relative to drefs feem to have entirely changed fince Lady Mary's time, and if the drefs of the ladies be ftill as abfurd, it is at leaft not fo fingular; for they, like the reft of Europe, have now adopted the Parifian modes.

The prefént race of Auftrian ladies can differ in nothing more than they do in looks from their grandmothers, who, if any of them

them were ftill alive, may be as beautiful at
this day as they were when fhe wrote; for
time itfelf could hardly improve that ugli-
nefs, which, according to her, was in full
bloom fixty years ago. I have not as yet
enquired what method the parents have de-
vifed to remedy this inconveniency; but
nothing is more certain than that it is reme-
died very effectually; for at prefent there is
no fcarcity of female beauty at the court of
Vienna.

This being the cafe, it is natural to imagine that gallantry muft now be more prevalent than when her ladyfhip was here.
But exclufive of any real difference, which
may have happened in the fentiments of the
ladies themfelves, they are obliged to obferve
an uncommon degree of circumfpection in
that particular, as nothing is more heinous
in the eyes of her Imperial Apoftolic Majefty. She feems to think that the ladies
of her court, like the wife of Cæfar, fhould
not only be free from guilt, but, what is

ftill

ftill more difficult, free from fufpicion; and
ftrongly marks by her manner, that fhe is
but too well informed when any piece of
fcandal circulates to the prejudice of any of
them.

With regard to what Lady Mary calls fub-
marriages, and of which fhe has given fuch
a curious account, I do not imagine they are
common at prefent, in all the latitude of her
defcription. But it is not uncommon for
married ladies here to avow the greateft degree of friendfhip and attachment to men
who are not their hufbands, and to live with
them in great intimacy, without hurting
their reputation, or being fufpected, even
by their own fex, of having deviated from
the laws of modefty.

One evening at the Count Thune's, when
there was a pretty numerous company, I
obferved one lady uncommonly fad, and enquired of her intimate friend, who happened
to be there alfo, if fhe knew the caufe of this
fadnefs?

fadnefs?—I do, replied fhe; Mr. de ———,
whom fhe loves very tenderly, ought to have
been here a month ago; and laft night fhe
received a letter from him, informing her
that he cannot be at Vienna for a month to
come. But pray, faid I, does your friend's
hufband know of this violent paffion fhe has
for Mr. de ———? Yes, yes, anfwered fhe,
he knows it, and enters with the moft tender fympathy into her affliction; he does
all that can be expected from an affectionate
hufband to comfort and foothe his wife,
affuring her that her love will wear away
with time. But fhe always declares that
fhe has no hopes of this, becaufe fhe feels
it augment every day.—Mais, au fond, continued the lady, cela lui fait bien de la peine,
parceque malheureufement il aime fa femme
à la folie. Et fa femme, qui eft la meil-
leure créature du monde, plaint infiniment
fon pauvre mari; car elle a beaucoup d'ami-
tié et d'eftime pour lui;—mais elle ne fçau-

roit

roit fe défaire de cette malheureufe paffion
pour Monf. de ————.

I was not in the leaft furprifed that a difappointment of this nature fhould affect a
woman a little; but I own it did aftonifh
me that fhe fhould appear in public, on
fuch an occafion, in all the oftentation of
forrow, like a young widow vain of her
weeds. Here this paffion was lamented by
her friends as a misfortune: In England, if
I rightly remember, fuch misfortunes are
generally imputed to people as crimes.

LETTER LXXXVII.

Prefburg.

THE Vifcount de Laval having propofed to me lately to make a fhort
tour with him into Hungary, I very readily confented, and we arrived at this town
yefterday morning.

Prefburg, which is the capital of Lower
Hungary, like Vienna, has fuburbs more
magnificent than itfelf. In this city the
States of Hungary hold their affemblies,
and in the cathedral church the Sovereign
is crowned.

The prefent Emprefs took refuge here
when the Elector of Bavaria was declared
Emperor at Prague, when fhe was abandoned
by her allies, and when France had planned
her deftruction. Her own magnanimity,

Y 3   the

the generous friendfhip of Great Britain, and the courage of her Hungarian fubjects, at length reftored her fortunes, and fecured to her family the fplendid fituation they now hold in Europe.

What politician in 1741 could have thought, that in the courfe of a few years the Emprefs would be in ftrict alliance with France, and one of her daughters feated on the throne of that kingdom?—Should a foothfayer of Bofton prophefy, that John Hancock, or his fon, will, fome time hence, demand in marriage a daughter of England,—pray, do not lay an uncommon odds, that the thing will not happen.

Monf. de Laval and I walked up this morning to the caftle, which is a noble Gothic building, of a fquare form, with a tower at each corner. The regalia of Hungary, confifting of the crown and fceptre of St. Stephen, the firft king, are depofited here. Thefe are carefully fecured by feven locks, the keys of which are kept by the
same

fame number of Hungarian noblemen. No Prince is held by the populace as legally their Sovereign till he be crowned with the diadem of King Stephen; and they have a notion that the fate of their nation depends on this crown's remaining in their poffef-fion. It has therefore been always removed in times of danger to places of the greateft fafety.

The Turks, aware of the influence of fuch a prejudice in the minds of the vulgar, have, it is faid, made frequent attempts to feize this Palladium.—The fate of Hungary feems now to be pretty much decided; fo that ex-clufive of the value they put upon the crown, as a relic of confiderable antiquity, the Hungarians need not be folicitous whether it remains in this caftle or in the Imperial palace at Vienna.

By the conftitution of Hungary, the crown is ftill held to be elective. This point is not difputed. All that is infift-ed on is, that the heir of the Houfe of Au-

Y 4

ftria

ftria fhall be elected as often as a vacancy happens.

The caftle of Prefburg is the ufual refidence of Prince Albert of Saxony, who married one of the Arch-ducheffes, a very beautiful and accomplifhed Princefs. As M. de Laval and I entered one of the rooms, we obferved them at a window. We immediately ftarted back, and withdrew, being in riding frocks and boots. Monf. de Laval had feen their Highneffes a few days before at Schonbrun, and thought they had been there ftill. The Princefs fent a polite meffage after us by a fervant, who had orders to conduct us through every apartment of the caftle; fhe herfelf ftept into another room, that we might fee that which fhe left.

All the Princeffes of the Auftrian family are diftinguifhed by an attentive and obliging politenefs, which is the more remarkable, as thofe who live much at courts often acquire a fpecies of politenefs which is by no
means

means obliging. The splendor and distinctions of a court frequently inspire an overweening vanity, and have a peculiar tendency to shake the steadiness of the female understanding. Court ladies in general, but particularly such as submit to be abject sycophants to Queens and Princesses, are apt to render themselves ridiculous by the arrogant airs they assume to the rest of the world, and while they usurp the importance of royalty, fill the breasts of all who know them with as much detestation as is consistent with contempt.

The view from this citadel is very extensive, commanding the vast and fertile plains of Hungary.

Having dined at the inn, and regaled ourselves, at no great expence, with tokay, we went to visit a villa at the distance of four miles from Presburg, belonging to a Hungarian nobleman. This house is delightfully situated,—the gardens laid out a little too methodically;—but the park, and

8   fields

fields around, where lefs art has been ufed, difplay a vaft luxuriancy of natural beauties. —While wandering over thefe, we entered a little wood in a very retired place; as we advanced into this, we faw a venerable look-ing old man with a long beard, who, ftretching out his hand, feemed to invite us to an hermitage which we obferved hard by.

The Vifcount, impatient to cultivate the acquaintance of a perfon of fuch an hofpi-table appearance, ran before me toward him; when he got up to him, he ftopped fhort as if furprifed, and then, to my utter aftonifh-ment he raifed his foot with every mark of indignation, and gave the poor old hermit a violent kick.

I do not remember that I was ever more fhocked in my life; I was at the fame time quite confounded at an action fo unworthy in itfelf, and fo incompatible with the cha-racter of Monf. de Laval.—I was foon re-conciled, however, to the treatment the old
fellow

fellow had received, when I difcovered that
this venerable perfonage was not the honeft
man we took him for, but a downright im-
poftor, made of painted wood, and dreffed
in the robes of a hermit to deceive paffengers.

Over the door was an infcription from
Horace——

 Odi profanum vulgus *.

On the infide of the door——

 Fata volentes ducunt, nolentes †.

And in another part, within the hermitage——

 Omnes eodem cogimur; omnium
 Verfatur urna, ferius ocius,
 Sors exitura, et nos in æternum
 Exilium impofitura Cymbæ ‡.

* I abhor the profane vulgar.
† Fate leads the willing, and drags the unwilling.
‡ Thus all muft tread the path of fate,
 Thus even fhakes the mortal urn,
 Whofe lot embarks us, foon or late,
 On Charon's boat, ah, never to return!
Francis.
There

There were alfo feveral infcriptions taken from Cicero, in favour of the foul's immortality, which I am forry I neglected to tranfcribe.—We returned in the evening to this place, and are to fet out to-morrow for Prince Eftherhafie's.

LETTER LXXXVIII.

Vienna.

HAVING left Prefburg, we travelled eight pofts acrofs a very fertile country to the palace of Eftherhafie, the refidence of the Prince of that name. He is the firft in rank of the Hungarian nobility, and one of the moft magnificent fubjects in Europe. He has body-guards of his own, all genteel-looking men, richly dreffed in the Hungarian manner.

The palace is a noble building, lately finifhed, and fituated near a fine lake. The apartments are equally grand and commodious: the furniture more fplendid than almoft any thing I have feen in royal palaces. In the Prince's own apartment there are

fome

some curious musical clocks, and one in the shape of a bird, which whistles a tune every hour.

Just by the palace, there is a theatre for operas, and other dramatic entertainments; and in the gardens, a large room with commodious apartments for masquerades and balls.

At no great distance, there is another theatre expressly built for puppet-shows. This is much larger and more commodious than most provincial playhouses, and I am bold to assert, is the most splendid that has as yet been reared in Europe for that species of actors. We regretted that we could not have the pleasure of seeing them perform; for they have the reputation of being the best comedians in Hungary.

We had the curiosity to peep behind the curtain, and saw Kings, Emperors, Turks, and Christians, all ranged very sociably together.—King Solomon was observed in a

corner

corner in a very fufpicious tête-a-tête with the Queen of Sheba.

Among other curiofities, there is in the garden a wooden houfe, built upon wheels. It contains a room with a table, chairs, a looking-glafs, chimney, and fire-place. There are alfo clofets, with many neceffary accommodations.—The Prince fometimes entertains twelve people in this vehicle, all of whom may eafily fit round the table, and the whole company may thus take an airing together along the walks of the garden, and many parts of the park, which are as level as a bowling-green. The machine, when thus loaded, is eafily drawn by fix or eight horfes.

Prince Eftherhafie having heard of M. de Laval's being in the garden, fent us an invitation to the opera, which was to be performed that evening; but as we had brought with us no drefs proper for fuch an occafion, we were forced to decline this obliging invitation. The Prince afterwards fent

a car-a carriage, in which we drove round the garden and parks. Thefe are of vaft extent, and beautiful beyond defcription; arbours, fountains, walks, woods, hills, and valleys, being thrown together in a charming confufion.—If you will look over Ariofto's defcription of the gardens in Alcina's inchanted ifland, you will have an idea of the romantic fields of Eftherhafie, which are alfo inhabited by the fame kind of animals.

> Tra le purpuree rofe e i bianchi gigli,
> Cha tepid aura frefchi ognora ferba,
> Sicuri fi vedean lepri e conigli:
> E cervi con la fronte alta e fuperba,
> Senza temer che alcun li uccida o pigli,
> Pafcono, e ftanfi ruminando l'erba:
> E Saltan daini e capri fnelli e deftri,
> Che fono in copia in quei luoghi campeftri*.

M. de

* While 'midft the rofes red and lilies fair,
For ever nurs'd by kindly zephyr's care,
The nimble hares, in wanton mazes play'd,
And ftately ftags with branching antlers ftray'd;
Without the fear of hoftile hand, they ftood
To crop, or ruminate their graffy food.

The

M. de Laval was in raptures with the gardens of Eftherhafie. In the height of his admiration, I afked him, how they ftood in his opinion, compared with thofe of Verfailles?

Ah, Parbleu! Monfieur, anfwered he, Verfailles étoit fait exprès pour n'être comparé à rien.—He acknowledged, however, with difficulty, that, except France, no other country he had feen was fo beautiful as this.

Having wandered here many hours, we returned to the inn, where a fervant waited with Prince Eftherhafie's compliments, and a bafket containing two bottles of Tokay, and the fame quantity of Champaign and of Old Hock. We lamented very fincerely, that we could not have the honour of waiting on this very magnificent Prince, and thanking him perfonally for fo much politenefs.

> The wild goats frolick; leap the nimble deer,
> That in this rural place in troops appear.

A com-

A company of Italian fingers and actors were then at the inn, and preparing for the opera. Great preparations were making for the entertainment of the Emprefs and all the Court, who are foon to make a vifit of feveral days to Eftherhafie. Though the Imperial family, and many of the nobility, are to lodge in the palace, yet every corner of this large and commodious inn is already befpoke for the company which are invited upon that occafion.

Hungary is a very cheap country, the land being infinitely fertile, and in fome places producing the moft efteemed grape in Europe. It is beautiful with lakes, the windings of the Danube, and many ftreams which flow into that fine river. In the woods of Hungary are bred a race of horfes, the moft active, hardy, and fpirited, for their fize, in the world. Thefe have been found very ufeful in war, and the huffars, or light dragoons of the Auftrian army, are mounted on them.

The

The men in Hungary are remarkably handſome, and well-ſhaped. Their appearance is improved by their dreſs, which you know is peculiar, and very becoming.

Lady M. W. Montague aſſerts, that the Hungarian women are far more beautiful than the Auſtrian. For my part, I think of women, as M. de Laval does of Verſailles;—that they are not to be compared with any thing,—not even with one another. And therefore, without preſuming to take a comparative view of their beauty, it may be remarked in general, that where the men are handſome and well-made, it is natural to ſuppoſe, that the women will poſſeſs the ſame advantages; for parents generally beſtow as much attention to the making of their daughters as of their ſons. In confirmation of which doctrine, I can aſſure you, that I have ſeen as handſome women, as men, in Hungary, and one of the prettieſt women, in my opinion,

Z 2

at

at prefent at the Court of Vienna, is a
Hungarian.

None of the Emprefs's fubjects are taxed
fo gently, or enjoy fo many privileges as
the Hungarians. This is partly owing to
the grateful remembrance fhe has of their
loyalty and attachment in the days of her
diftrefs. But although this fentiment were
not fo ftrong in her breaft as it really is,
there are political reafons for continuing to
them the fame exemptions and privileges;
for nothing can be more dangerous than dif-
obliging the inhabitants of a frontier country, which borders on an inveterate enemy.
—Nor could any thing pleafe the Turks
more, than to find the hearts of the Hungarians alienated from the houfe of Auftria.

I found this country, and the company
of M. de Laval, fo very agreeable, that I
fhould have been happy to have extended
our excurfion farther; but he is obliged to

fet

fet out foon for Chamberry to pay his duty to the Comte d'Artois, who is expected there to wait on his future fpoufe, the Princefs of Savoy. We therefore returned by the direct road from Eftherhafie to Vienna.

LETTER LXXXIX.

SO the fate of poor ——— is finally decided, and he now finds, that to be ruined
is not a matter of fo much indifference as
he once imagined. I neither fee the poffibility of his extricating himfelf from his
prefent difficulties, nor in what manner he
will be able to fupport them. Accuftomed
to every luxuriant indulgence, how can
he bear the inconveniencies of poverty?—
Diffipated and inattentive from his childhood, how can he make any exertion for
himfelf?—His good-humour, genteel figure,
and pliant difpofition, made him well received by all.—While he formed no expectations from their friendfhip, his company feemed particularly acceptable to fome
who

who are at prefent in power: Whether it
will be equally fo now, when he has nothing elfe to depend on, is to be tried.
And I really think it as well for him
that it be tried now, as five or fix years
hence.

᠂ This calamity has been long forefeen.—
There feemed to be almoft a neceffity that
it fhould happen fooner or later; for he
had neither caution, plan, nor object in his
gaming.—He continued it from habit
alone. Of all mankind, he was the leaft
covetous of exceffive wealth; and exclufive
of gaming, he always lived within his income, not from a defire of faving money,
but merely becaufe he had no tafte for great
expence.—How often have we feen him
lofe immenfe fums to thofe who could never
have paid the half, had he happened to
win it; and to fome of whom he had
lent the money which enabled them to
ftake againft him?

Z 4

There

There are many carelefs young men of great fortunes, who game in the fame ftyle, and from no other motives than thofe of our unhappy friend.—What is the confequence?—The money circulates for a while among them, but remains finally with perfons of a very different character.—I fhall not fuppofe that any of the very fortunate gamefters we have been acquainted with, have ufed thofe means to correct fortune which are generally reckoned fraudulent. I am fully per-fuaded, they are feldomer practifed in the clubs in London, than in any other gam-ing focieties in the world.—Let all flight of hand, and every fpecies of downright fharping, be put out of the queftion; but ftill we may fuppofe, that among a great number of carelefs inattentive people of fortune, a few wary, cool, and fhrewd men are mingled, who know how to con-ceal real caution and defign under appa-rent inattention and gaiety of manner;—

who

who have a perfect command of themfelves, pufh their luck when fortune fmiles,
and refrain when fhe changes her difpofition;—who have calculated the chances,
and underftand every game where judgment is required.

If there are fuch men, is not the probability of winning infinitely in their favour?—Does it not amount to almoft as
great a certainty, as if they had actually
loaded the dice or packed the cards?—I
know you live in the habit of intimacy
with fome who anfwer to the above defcription; and I have heard you fay, that
however fortunate they may have been,
you were fully convinced that nothing
can be fairer than their manner of playing.
I accufe them of taking no other advantages
than thofe above-mentioned; but I appeal
to your own experience,—pray recollect,—
and I am greatly miftaken, if you will not
find, that by far the greater part of thofe
who have made fortunes by play, and
have

have kept them when made, are men of cool, cautious, fhrewd, and felfifh cha-racters.

If any of thefe very fortunate people were brought to a trial, and examined by what means they had accumulated fuch fums, while fo many others had entirely loft, or greatly impaired their fortunes (if the word efprit be allowed to imply that artful fuperiority which belongs to their characters), they might anfwer in the words of the wife of Concini Marechal d'Ancre, when fhe was afked what charm fhe had made ufe of to fafcinate the mind of the Queen?—De l'afcendant, fhe re-plied, qu'un efprit fuperieur a toujours fur des efprits foibles.—Certainly there can be no greater weaknefs, than for a man of independent fortune to game in fuch a manner as to rifk lofing it, for the chance of doubling or tripling his income: be-caufe the additional happinefs arifing from any fuppofable addition of wealth, can

never

never be within a thoufand degrees fo great, as the mifery which would be the confequence of his being ftripped of his original fortune.

This confideration alone, one would imagine, might be fufficient to deter any reafonable man from a conduct fo weak and abfurd: yet there are other confiderations which give much additional weight to the argument:—the difmal effects which the continued practice of gaming has fometimes been obferved to produce in the difpofition of the mind, and the moft effential parts of the character, deftroying every idea of œconomy, engroffing the whole time, undermining the beft principles, perverting the qualities of the heart, rendering men callous to the ruin of acquaintances, and partakers, with a favage infenfibility, in the fpoils of their unwary friends.

The

The peculiar inftances with which you and I are acquainted, where the long-continued habit of deep play has had no fuch effects, are proofs of the rooted honour and integrity of certain individuals, and may ferve as exceptions to a general rule, but cannot be urged as arguments againft the ufual tendency of gaming. If men of fortune and character adopted the practice of gaming upon any principle of reafoning, there might be a greater probability of their being reafoned out of it: but moft of them begin to game, not with any view or fixed plan of increafing their wealth, but merely as a fafhionable amufement, or perhaps by way of fhowing the liberality of their fpirit, and their contempt for money.

I would not be very pofitive, that fome of them have not miftaken for admiration, that furprife which is expreffed when any perfon has loft an immenfe fum. And this

miftake

miſtake may have given them leſs repug-
nance to the idea of becoming the objects of
admiration in the ſame way. Afterwards
endeavouring to win back what they had
ſo idly loſt, the habit has grown by degrees, and at length has become their ſole
reſource from the wearineſs which thoſe
born to great fortunes, and who have not
early in life acquired ſome faculty of amuſing themſelves, are more prone to fall into than others. Men born to no ſuch expectations, whatever their natural diſpoſi-
tions may be, are continually rouſed from
indolence by avocations which admit of
no delay. The purſuit of that independence, for which almoſt every human bo-
ſom ſighs, and whoſe value is unknown
only to thoſe who have always poſſeſſed it,
is thought a neceſſary, and is often found,
an agreeable employment to the generality
of mankind. This, with the other duties
of life, is ſufficient to engroſs their time
and

and thoughts, and guard them from *the pains and penalties of idleness.*

As the purfuit of wealth is fuperfluous in men of rank and fortune, fo it would be unbecoming their fituation. Being deprived of this, which is fo great an object and refource to the reft of mankind, they ftand in more need of fomething to fupply its place. I know of nothing which can fo completely, and with fo much propriety, have this effect, as a tafte for letters and love of fcience. I therefore think thefe are more effentially neceffary to the happinefs of people of high rank and great fortune, than to thofe in confined circumftances.

If independence be defired with univerfal ardour by mankind, the road of fcience is neither the moft certain, nor the fhorteft way to attain it. But thofe who are already in poffeffion of this, have infinite need of the other to teach them to enjoy
their

their independence with dignity and fatif-
faction, and to prevent the gifts of fortune
from becoming fources of mifery inftead of
happinefs.   If they are ambitious, the cultivation of letters, by adorning their minds,
and enlarging their faculties, will facilitate
their plans, and render them more fit for
the high fituations to which they afpire.
If they are devoid of ambition, they have
ftill more occafion for fome of the purfuits
of fcience, as refources againft the languor
of retired or inactive life.—Quod fi non hic
tantus fructus oftenderetur, et fi ex his ftudiis
delectatio fola peteretur; tamen, ut opinor,
hanc animi remiffionem, humaniffimam ac
liberaliffimam judicaretis.

This love of letters, confidered merely as
an amufement, and to fill up agreeably
the vacant hours of life, I believe to be
more effentially neceffary to men of great
fortune than to thofe who have none;—to
men without ambition, than to thofe who
are animated by that active paffion; and to
the

the generality of Englifhmen more than to
the natives of either Germany or France.—
The Germans require very little variety.
They can bear the languid uniformity of
life always with patience, and often with
fatisfaction. They difplay an equanimity
under difguft that is quite aftonifhing.—
The French, though not fo celebrated for
patience, are of all mankind the leaft liable
to defpondence. Public affairs, fo apt to
difturb the repofe of many worfhipful citizens of London, never give a Frenchman
uneafinefs. If the arms of France are fuc-
cefsful, he rejoices with all his heart;—if
they are unfortunate, he laughs at the commanders with all his foul. If his miftrefs
is kind, he celebrates her goodnefs, and com-
mends her tafte;—if fhe is cruel, he derides
her folly in the arms of another.

No people ever were fo fond of amufement, and fo eafily amufed. It feems to
be the chief object of their lives, and they
contrive to draw it from a thoufand fources,

4

.in

in which no other people ever thought it could be found. I do not know where I met with the following lines; they are natural and easy, and seem expressive of the conduct and sentiments of the whole French nation.

> M'amuser n'importe comment;
> Fait toute ma philosophie.
> Je crois ne perdre aucun moment
> Hors le moment où je m'ennuie;
> Et je tiens ma tâche finie.
> Pourvu qu'ainsi tout doucement;
> Je me defasse de la vie.

Our countrymen who have applied to letters, have prosecuted every branch of science as successfully as any of their neighbours. But those of them who study mere amusement, independent of literature of any kind, certainly have not been so happy in their researches as the French. Many things which entertain the latter, seem frivolous and insipid to the former. The English view objects through a darker

medium. Lefs touched than their neighbours with the gaieties, they are more affected by the vexations of life, under which
they are too ready to defpond. They feel
their fpirits flag with the repetition of
fcenes which at firft were thought agreeable. This ftagnation of animal fpirits,
from whatever, caufe it arifes, becomes itfelf a caufe of defperate refolutions, and
debafing habits.

A man of fortune, therefore, who can
acquire fuch a relifh for fcience, as will
make him rank its purfuits among his
amufements, has thereby made an acquifition of more importance to his happinefs,
than if he had acquired another eftate equal
in value to his firft. I am almoft convinced, that a tafte of this kind is the only
thing which can render a man of fortune
(efpecially if his fortune be very large) to-
lerably independent and eafy through life.
Whichfoever of the roads of fcience he
loves to follow, his curiofity will continually

nually be kept awake. An inexhauftible variety of interefting objects will open to his
view,—his mind will be replenifhed with
ideas,—and even when the purfuits of ambition become infipid, he will ftill have an-
tidotes againft tædium, and (other things
being fuppofed equal) the beft chance of
paffing agreeably through life, that the uncertainty of human events allows to man.

A a 2

LETTER XC.

Vienna.

IN your laft, you fhow fuch a paffion for anecdote, and feem fo defirous of my infifting on manners and chara&ers, that I fear you will not be pleafed with my laft long epiftle upon a fubjeƈt entirely remote from what you demand.   But you muft remember, that you were warned from the beginning of this correfpondence, that I would retain the privilege of digreffing as often as I pleafed, and that my letters fl.ould frequently treat of what I thought, as well as what I faw.   However, this fhall confift entirely of fights.

The firft I fhall mention was exhibited foon after our arrival at Vienna.   This was
the.

the feaſt of St. Stephen, at which the Emperor dined in public with the knights.

He was at the head of the table; his brother and brother-in law next him, and the other knights ſat according to ſeniority. The Arch-ducheſſes, with ſome of the principal ladies of the court, were at a balcony within the hall to ſee this ceremony.—The Emperor and all the knights were dreſſed in the robes of the order. The Hungarian guards, with their ſabres drawn, ſurrounded the table.

The honour of ſerving the Emperor at this ſolemnity belongs entirely to the Hungarians. When he called for drink, a Hungarian nobleman poured a little of the wine into a cup and taſted it; he afterwards filled another, which he preſented with one knee touching the ground. The Emperor often ſmiled upon this nobleman as he went through the ceremony, and ſeemed to indicate, by the whole of his

A a 3   behaviour,

behaviour, that he confidered fuch fubmif-
five bendings of one man to another, as
greatly mifplaced, and that he fuffered this
mummery merely in compliance with ancient cuftom.

There was great crowding to fee this
feaft, and it was not without difficulty
I got admiffion; though, after all, there
was nothing to be feen but fome well-
dreffed men, who ate an exceeding good
dinner with tolerable appetite.

Since the feaft of St. Stephen, we have
been witneffes to the annual ceremony in
commemoration of the defeat of the Turk-
ifh army, and the raifing the fiege of Vienna by John Sobiefki king of Poland.
The Imperial family, and the principal nobility of both fexes, walked in folemn proceffion, and heard mafs at the church of
St. Stephen on this occafion. In the
middle of the ftreet, leading from the
palace to the church, a platform was
raifed, upon which the company, who
formed

formed the proceffion, walked.—The ftreets were lined with the Imperial guards, and the windows and tops of the houfes were crowded with fpectators.—The Duke of Hamilton and I found a very good fituation at a window with the Venetian ambaffador.

This ceremony would have been too fatiguing for the Emprefs:—She therefore did not attend:—The Emperor, the Archdukes and Ducheffes, with all the nobility, did. A prodigious train of bifhops, priefts, and monks followed; and a numerous band of mufic played as they went along.

As this is a day of rejoicing, the richeft and gayeft dreffes are thought the moft expreffive of the pious gratitude becoming fuch an occafion. The ladies difplayed their devotion in the moft brilliant manner. Their minds, however, were not fo much exalted by heavenly contemplations, as to be above taking notice of their earthly acquaintances at the windows, whom they

regaled

regaled with fmiles and nods as they walked along.

Next day the Imperial family dined in public, and many people went to fee them. I was not of the number, though nobody can more fincerely wifh them the enjoyment of all the comforts of life. I know not on what principle the Royal Family in France, and other countries in Europe, have adopted the cuftom of eating in public. They cannot imagine, that the feeing them chew and fwallow their victuals can create a vaft deal of admiration in the beholders. It would certainly be taken for granted, that they could perform thefe neceffary functions, although a cloud of witneffes were not admitted to confirm the fact. If thefe exhibitions are defigned for the entertainment of the fubjects, a thoufand could be thought of more amufing to them; for however interefting the part of an actor at a feaft may be, that of a

fpectator

fpectator is furely one of the moft infipid that can be imagined.

But the fame evening there was a grand mafquerade at Schonbrun, which was more generally amufing.—Four thoufand tickets were diftributed on this occafion.——A large party of dragoons were placed along the road from Vienna, to keep the coaches in a regular line, and to prevent confufion. The principal rooms of this magnificent palace were thrown open for the reception of the company. In three large halls on the ground-floor, tables were covered with a cold collation of all kinds of fowls, ham, and confections, with pine apples and every fort of fruit. Thefe, with Old Hock, Champagne, and other kinds of wine, were ferved with readinefs and profufion to all who afked for them.

At the end of the large dining room, there was a raifed feat for the Emprefs, and fome ladies who attended her. Here
a grand

a grand Ballet was danced by the Arch-duke, the Arch-ducheſſes, the Princeſs of Modena, and ſome of the chief nobi-lity, to the number of twenty-four. The dancers, both male and female, were dreſſed in white ſilk, flounced with pink-coloured ribbands, and enriched with a vaſt profuſion of diamonds.

This ballet was performed three times at proper intervals. Thoſe who had ſeen it once, paſſed into the gallery, and other apartments, giving way to a new ſet of ſpectators. In the garden, on a riſing ground oppoſite to the palace windows, a temporary fabric was erected in the form of a large and magnificent temple. This was illuminated by an incredible number of lamps, and gave the appearance of a very extraordinary piece of architecture, which continued flaming through the whole night, and had a very fine effect, viewed from Vienna, and other places at a greater diſtance,

The

The Emperor mixed with the company without ceremony or diftinction, taking no part himfelf but as a fpectator. He was converfing in the middle of the hall, in the moft familiar manner, with an Englifh gentleman, without obferving, that the third ballet was going to be danced, when the mafter of the ceremonies whifpered him in the ear.—The Emperor, feizing the Englifhman by the arm, faid, Allons, Monfieur, on nous chaffe—il faut fe retirer; and immediately walked into another room, to give place to others who had not yet feen the dance.

This very fplendid entertainment was given to the Arch-duke, and the Princefs of Modena, whofe ufual refidence is at Milan.—The Emprefs, thus furrounded by her offspring, appeared cheerful and happy.—She feemed to enjoy the vivacity, and fympathife with the gaiety, of the company.—She is greatly beloved by her own children, and by her fubjects in general,

whom

whom fhe alfo confiders as her children in a greater degree than is ufual for fovereigns.

It is an error to imagine, that great devotion has a tendency to four the temper: Though it muft be acknowledged, that it has not always the power of fweetening the very auftere trunks on which it is fometimes grafted; but in a character naturally benevolent, every good difpofition will be ftrengthened and animated by real piety. Of this I have feen a thoufand inftances, and I believe her Imperial Majefty affords one.

LETTER XCI.

Vienna.

THE Emperor is of a middle fize, well made, and of a fair complexion. He has a confiderable refemblance to his fifter, the Queen of France, which, in my opinion, is faying a great deal in favour of his looks.—Till I faw fomething of his ufual behaviour, I did not think it poffible for a perfon, in fuch an elevated fituation, to put every body with whom he converfed upon fo eafy a footing.

His manner, as I have often mentioned, is affable, obliging, and perfectly free from the referved and lofty deportment affumed by fome on account of high birth. Who-ever has the honour to be in company with him, fo far from being checked by fuch defpicable

defpicable pride, has need to be on his guard, not to adopt fuch a degree of familiarity as, whatever the condefcenfion of the one might permit, would be highly improper in the other to ufe.

He is regular in his way of life, moderate in his pleafures, fteady in his plans, and diligent in bufinefs. He is fond of his army, and inclines that the foldiers fhould have every comfort and neceffary confiftent with their fituation. He is certainly an œconomift, and lavifhes very little money on ufelefs pomp, miftreffes, or favourites; and it is, I fuppofe, on no better foundation than this, that his enemies accufe him of avarice.

I cannot help regarding œconomy as one of the moft ufeful qualities in a Prince. Liberality, even when pufhed to an imprudent length, may, in a private perfon, proceed from a kind of greatnefs of mind, becaufe his fortune is in every fenfe his own, and he can injure nobody but himfelf by

lavifhing

lavifhing it away—He knows that when it is gone, nobody will reimburfe him for his extravagance.—He feems therefore to have taken the refolution to fubmit to the inconveniency of future poverty, rather than renounce the prefent happinefs of acting with a magnificent liberality, and beftowing on others more than he can afford.

This is not the cafe with a Prince.— What he fquanders is not his own, but the public money.—He knows that his pomp and fplendour will be kept up, and that his fubjects, not he, are to feel the inconveniencies of his prodigality. When I hear, therefore, that a King has given great fums of money to any particular perfon ; from the fums given, the perfon who receives it, the motive for the gift, and other circumftances, I can judge whether it is well or ill difpofed of ; but in either, cafe, it cannot be called generofity.

The virtue of generofity confifts in a man's depriving himfelf of fomething for

S   the

the fake of another. There can be no generofity in giving to John what James
muft replace the next moment. What is
called generofity in Kings, very often confifts in beftowing that money on the idle
part· of their fubjects which they have
fqueezed from the induftrious. I have
heard a parcel of fiddlers and opera dancers
praife a Prince for his noble and generous
behaviour to them, while men near his
perfon, of ufeful talents and real worth,
were diftreffed for bread.—The Emperor certainly has none of that kind of generofity.

His ufual drefs (the only one indeed in
which I ever faw him, except at the feaft
of the Knights of St. Stephen) is a plain
uniform of white faced with red.—When
he goes to Laxenberg, Schonbrun, and
other places near Vienna, he generally
drives two horfes in an open chaife, with
a fervant behind, and no other attendant
of any kind.—He very feldom allows the
guard to turn out as he paffes through the
gate,

gate.—Nobody ever had a ſtronger diſpoſition to judicious inquiry.—He is fond of
converſing with ingenious people.—When
he hears of any perſon, of whatever rank
or country, being diſtinguiſhed for any
particular talent, he is eager to converſe
with him, and turns the converſation to
the ſubjeᴄt on which that perſon is thought
to excel, drawing from him all the uſeful
information he can. Of all the means of
knowledge, this is perhaps the moſt powerful, and the moſt proper that can be uſed,
by one whoſe more neceſſary occupations
do not leave him much time for ſtudy.

He ſeems to be of opinion, that the vanity and ignorance of many Princes are
frequently owing to the forms in which
they are intrenched, and to their being deprived of the advantages which the reſt of
mankind enjoy from a free compariſon
and exchange of ſentiment. He is convinced, that unleſs a King can contrive to
live in ſome ſocieties on a footing of equa-

VOL. II.　　　B b　　　　　lity,

lity, and can weigh his own merit, without throwing his guards and pomp into the fcale, it will be difficult for him to know either the world or himfelf.

One evening at the Countefs Walftein's, the converfation leading that way, the Emperor enumerated fome remarkable and ludicrous inftances of the inconveniencies of etiquette, which had occurred at a certain court. One perfon prefent hinted at the effectual means his Majefty had ufed to banifh every inconveniency of that kind from the Court of Vienna. To which he replied, It would be hard indeed, if, becaufe I have the ill-fortune to be an Emperor, I fhould be deprived of the pleafures of focial life, which are fo much to my tafte. All the grimace and parade to which people in my fituation are accuftomed from their cradle, have not made me fo vain, as to imagine that I am in any effential quality fuperior to other men ; and if I had any tendency to fuch an opinion, the fureft way

ot

to get rid of it, is the method I take, of
mixing in fociety, where I have daily occafions of finding myfelf inferior in talents to
thofe I meet with. Confcious of this, it
would afford me no enjoyment to affume
airs of a fuperiority which I feel does not
exift. I endeavour therefore to pleafe, and
to be pleafed; and as much as the inconveniency of my fituation will permit, to enjoy the bleffings of fociety like other men,
convinced that the man who is fecluded
from thofe, and raifes himfelf above friendfhip, is alfo raifed above happinefs, and deprived of the means of acquiring knowledge.

This kind of language is not uncommon with poor philofophers; but I imagine it is rarely held by Princes, and the
inferences to be drawn from it more rarely
put in practice.

A few days after this, there was an exhibition of fire-works on the Prater. This

is

is a large park, planted with wood, and furrounded by the Danube, over which there is a wooden bridge. No carriages being allowed to pafs, the company leave their coaches at one end, and walk. There is a narrow path railed off on one fide of the bridge. Many people very injudicioufly took this path, to which there is an eafy entrance at one end, but the exit is difficult at the other; for only one perfon can go out at a time. The path therefore was very foon choaked up; the unfortunate paffengers crept on at a fnail's pace, and in the moft ftraitened and difagreeable manner imaginable; whilft thofe who had kept the wide path in the middle of the bridge, like the fortunate and wealthy in their journey through life, moved along at their eafe, totally regardlefs of the wretched circumftances of their fellow-paffengers.

Some few of the prifoners in the narrow paffage who were of a fmall fize, and
uncom-

uncommon addrefs, crawled under the rail, and got into the broad walk in the middle; but all who were tall, and of a larger make, were obliged to remain and fubmit to their fate. An Englifhman, who had been at the Countefs Walftein's when the Emperor exprefled himfelf as above mentioned, was of the laft clafs. The Emperor, as he pafled, feeing that thofe of a fmall fize extricated themfelves, while the Englifhman remained fixed in a very awkward fituation, called out, Ah, Monfieur! Je vous aie bien annoncé combien il eft incommode d'être trop *grand.*—A prefent vous devez être bien de mon avis;—Mais comme je ne puis rien faire pour vous foulager, je vous recommende à Saint George.

There are people, who having heard of the Emperor's uncommon affability, and of his total contempt of pomp and parade, of which the bulk of mankind are fo much enamoured, have afferted, that

the

the whole is affectation. But if the whole tenor of any perfon's words and actions is to be confidered as affectation, I do not know by what means we are to get at the bottom of his real character. Yet, people who have a violent tafte for any particular thing, are extremely ready to believe, that thofe who have not the fame tafte are affected.

I do not remember that I ever told you, that our friend R———, who loves his bottle above all things, and who, I believe, efteems you above all men, let me into a part of your character of which I never had the fmalleft fufpicion.

One day after dinner, when a couple of bottles had awakened his friendfhip, and laid open his heart, he took it into his head to enumerate your good qualities, and concluded the lift, by faying, that you were no milk-fop.—I know what that expreffion imports in the mouth of R———. I

therefore

therefore ſtared, and ſaid, I had ſeldom
ſeen you drink above three glaſſes at a time
in my life.—Nor I, ſaid he; but take my
word for it, he is too honeſt a fellow not
to love good wine, and I am certain his
ſobriety is all *affectation.*

B b 4

LETTER XCII.

I Returned very lately from Prince Lichtenſtein's houſe at Felberg in Auſtria,
where I paſſed a few days very agreeably.
The Lichtenſtein family is one of the firſt
in this country, whether conſidered in
point of antiquity, wealth, or dignity. This
Prince, beſides his lands in Auſtria, has
conſiderable eſtates in Bohemia, Moravia,
and that part of Sileſia which belongs to
the Empreſs.   Like Prince Eſtherhaſie, he
has body guards in his own pay.—I believe
no other ſubjects in Europe retain this diſtinction.

Felberg is a fine old manſion, about forty
miles from Vienna.   The apartments are
large, convenient, and furniſhed in the
magni-

magnificent ſtyle which prevails in the noblemen's houſes of this country.   The
company conſiſted of the Prince and Princeſs, the Count Degenfeldt and his lady,
a very accompliſhed woman; the Duke of
Hamilton, Mr. Milnes an Engliſh officer,
another Engliſh gentleman, and myſelf.
Our entertainment was in every reſpect
ſplendid, particularly in the article of attendants.   Some of the Auſtrian nobility
carry this point of magnificence to a height,
which could ſcarcely be ſupported by the
beſt eſtates in England, where one footman
is more expenſive than four in this country.

The day after our arrival, breakfaſt was
ſerved to the company ſeparately in their
own apartments, as is the cuſtom here.
We afterwards ſet out for another villa
belonging to this Prince, at ſix miles diſtance, where he intended to give the Duke
the amuſement of hunting.   The Princeſs,
the Counteſs Degenfeldt, the Duke, and
Captain Milnes, were in one coach; the
Prince,

Prince, the Count, and I, in another; the two young Princes, with their governor and the young Englifh gentleman, in a third, with a great retinue on horfeback.

As the day was well advanced when we arrived, I imagined the hunting would begin immediately :—But every thing is done with method and good order in this country, and it was judged proper to dine in the firft place. This in due time being concluded, I thought the men would have proceeded directly to the fcene of action, leaving the ladies till their return.—But. here I found myfelf again miftaken :—The ladies were to affift in the whole of this expedition. But as there was a neceffity to traverfe a large wood, into which coaches could not enter, vehicles of a more commodious conftruction were prepared. I forget what name is given to thefe carriages. They are of the form of benches, with ftuffed feats, upon which fix or eight people may place themfelves one behind the other.

other. They are drawn by four horſes, and ſlide over the ground like a ſledge, paſſing along paths and tracklefs ways, over which no wheel-carriage could be drawn.

After being conveyed in this manner acrofs the wood, and a confiderable way beyond it, we came to a very large open field, in which there were ſeveral little circular inclofures of trees and underwood at wide intervals from each other.—This hunting had hitherto been attended with very little fatigue; for we had been carried the whole way in coaches, or on the ſledges, which are ſtill eaſier than any coach. In ſhort, we had been perfectly paſſive ſince breakfaſt, except during the time of dinner.

But when we arrived at this large plain, I was informed, that the hunting would commence within a very ſhort time. I then expected we ſhould have ſome yiolent exercife after ſo much inactivity, and began to fear that the ladies might be over-fatigued, when, lo! the Prince's ſervants

vants began to arrange some portable chairs at a small distance from one of the thickets above mentioned. The Princess, Countess, and the rest of the company took their places; and when every body was seated, they assured me that the hunting was just going to begin.

I own, my curiosity was now excited in a very uncommon degree; and I was filled with impatience to see the issue of a hunting, which had been conducted in a style so different from any idea I had of that diversion. While I sat lost in conjecture, I perceived, at a great distance, a long line of people moving towards the little wood, near which the company was seated. As they walked along, they gradually formed the segment of a circle, whose centre was this wood. I understood that these were peasants, with their wives and children, who, walking forward in this manner, rouse the game, which naturally take shelter in the thicket of trees and bushes. As

soon

foon as this happened, the peafants rufhed in at the fide oppofite to that where our company had taken poft, beat out the game, and then the maffacre began.

Each perfon was provided with a fufil, and many more were at hand loaded for immediate ufe. The fervants were employed in charging as faft as the pieces were fired off : So that an uninterrupted fhooting was kept up, as long as the game continued flying or running out of the wood.—The Prince hardly ever miffed.— He himfelf killed above thirty partridges, a few pheafants, and three hares.

At the beginning of this fcene, I was a good deal furprifed to fee a fervant hand a fufil to the Princefs, who with great coolnefs, and without rifing from her feat, took aim at a partridge, which immediately fell to the ground. With the fame eafe, fhe killed ten or twelve partridges and pheafants, at about double the number of fhots.—The execution done by the

8   reft

reſt of the company was by no means con‑ ſiderable.

Though I had not heard of it before, I now underſtood, that ſhooting is not an uncommon amuſement with the German ladies: And it is probable, their attention to the delicacy of the fair ſex, has induced the hardy Germans to render this diverſion ſo little fatiguing.

The company afterwards walked to other little incloſures of planting, where ſome game was driven out, and killed as before.—The following day, the Prince conducted us to another of his ſeats, where there is a very fine open wood, full of deer of every kind, ſome of them the largeſt I ever ſaw. There is alſo a great number of wild boars, one of which, by the Prince's permiſſion, the Duke of Hamilton killed.

Nothing could ſurpaſs the politeneſs and magnificence with which the company were entertained during the whole of their ſtay.

ftay. The Princefs is a woman of an amiable character, and a good underftanding; educates her children, and manages her affairs, with the utmoft prudence and propriety.

This family, and many of the nobility, who have hitherto been at their countryfeats, are now about to return to Vienna. The family of Monfieur and Madame de Pergen have been here for fome time. This lady is an intimate friend of the Countefs Thune; and nearly the fame company, who form her fociety, now affemble twice a week at the houfe of Madame de Pergen, who rivals the Countefs in good fenfe and many accomplifhments; and, without raifing jealoufy or ill-will, divides with her the efteem of the beft company of this place. The agreeable footing on which fociety is eftablifhed here, and the number of refpectable people with whom we are acquainted, fills me with regret at the thoughts of leaving Vienna; but the Duke of
Hamilton

Hamilton inclines to pafs the winter in Italy. Indeed, if he did not, he would be obliged to delay the journey a whole year, or fub-mit to the inconveniencies of travelling in the fummer months, which, in fo hot a climate, is rather to be avoided.

· LETTER XCIII.

I Have not faid any thing of the Auftrian army, having fome fufpicion that I rather over-dofed you with military details from Berlin, where the fubject of my letters was continually before my eyes. But the Emperor has very few of his troops in garrifon at Vienna. They make a fine appearance, and the army in general are more judicioufly clothed, than any other I have feen.

Inftead of coats with long fkirts, their uniform is a fhort jacket of white cloth, with waiftcoat and breeches of the fame; and each foldier has a furtout of coarfe grey cloth, which he wears in cold or rainy weather. This he rolls up in a very

VOL. II.   C c   fmall

fmall bulk when the weather is good, and it is little or no incumbrance on a march. They have fhort boots for fhoes; and, in place of hats, they wear caps of very ftout leather, with a brafs front, which ufually ftands up, but which may be let down upon occafion, to prevent their eyes from being incommoded by the fun.

Except a very few Hungarians who do duty within the palace, there are no troops in the Auftrian fervice with increafed pay, and exclufive privileges, under the denomination of body-guards; the marching regiments on the ordinary eftablifhment, form the garrifon of Vienna, and perform the duty of guards by rotation.

The infolence of the Prætorian bands at Rome, fo often terrible to their mafters; the frequent infurrections of the Janiffaries at Conftantinople, and the revolutions effected by the Ruffian guards at Peterfburgh, fufficiently point out the danger of fuch an inftitution. Thefe examples

8 may

may have influenced the Auftrian government to renounce a fyftem which feems to
render certain regiments. lefs ufeful, and
more dangerous, than the reft of the army.

The Auftrian army is calculated at confiderably above two hundred thoufand;
and it is imagined that there never was
a greater number of excellent officers in
the fervice than at prefent: fo that, in cafe of
a war with Pruffia, the two powers will be
more equally matched than ever. It would
be unfortunate for this Court if it fhould
break out at prefent; for there are fome
commotions among the peafants in Bohemia, which occafion a general difquiet,
and by which fome individuals have fuf-
tained great loffes. One nobleman of
the firft rank has had his houfe, and all the
furniture, burnt to the ground, together
with fome large out-houfes near his caftle.

Thefe exceffes, according to fome, proceed from mere wantonnefs, and love of
mifchief, in the people. Others affert,

that

that they are excited by the tyranny of the lords, which has driven thofe poor men to defpair. Whichfoever of thefe accounts is true, it feems evident to me, that it would be much better for the lords, as well as the peafants, that the latter, inftead of being bond-men, were in a ftate of freedom. At prefent, they pay their rent by working a certain number of days in the week for their mafters, and maintain themfelves and families by labouring the other days on their own account. You will readily believe, that more real bufinefs will be done in one day when they work for themfelves, than in two days labour for their lords. This occafions ill-humour and blows on the part of the mafter, and hatred and revolt on that of the peafants.

If the eftates in Bohemia were let to free-men at a reafonable rent, freedom and property would excite a fpirit of induftry among thefe indolent people. They would then work every day with cheerfulnefs and good

good will, and I am convinced the landlords revenues would increafe daily. In
confequence of this, the peafants would, in
all probability, continue as much attached
to the ground from choice, as they are at
prefent from neceffity.—Do we not fee families in Great Britain remain for many
generations on gentlemen's eftates, though
the mafter has the privilege of changing
his tenant, and the tenant his mafter, at
the end of every leafe?

In almoft every country in Europe, except England, the inhabitants are confined,
by fome barrier or other, to the fituation
in which they are born. The total want of
education neceffarily obliges the greater part
to gain their livelihood by bodily labour.
National opinions prevent others from ever
rifing above the level of their birth, however fublime their genius, or however great
their acquired knowledge. But in our ifland
the door of fcience, and confequently the
road to ambition, is open to almoft every

individual.

individual. Even in the moſt remote villages ſome degree of education is beſtowed on the pooreſt inhabitants.

This may be of little or no importance to ninety-nine in a hundred: and of the ſmall number who, by improving this pittance of knowledge, raiſe themſelves above the ſtate in which they were born, very few arrive at any degree of eminence; the reaſon of which is, that great genius is a quality very ſparingly dealt out to mankind. Though it muſt be allowed, that much the greater part of the inhabitants of the ſame country and climate are born with nearly the ſame natural abilities; and that the degrees of education, and other opportunities of improvement, gradually form all the difference which appears among them in after-life; yet I cannot, with Helvetius, believe that genius is entirely the work of education.

I am fully convinced, that Nature is continually producing ſome individuals in

every

every nation of a finer organization, with an infinitely greater aptitude for science of every kind, and whose minds are capable of a more sublime and extensive range of thought, than is attainable by the common run of mankind with any possible degree of culture. This natural superiority is what I call genius. Wherever a considerable share of this is lodged, a little cultivation will be sufficient, but some is absolutely requisite to make it appear.

When it does exist in the minds of peasants in Russia, Poland, and some parts of Germany, it remains dormant from neglect, or is smothered by oppression. But in Great Britain, the degree of education which is now universal, small as it is, will be sufficient to rouse, animate, and bring into action the fire of extraordinary genius, the seeds of which impartial Nature is as apt to place in the infant breast of a peasant as of a prince. The chance of great and distinguished men springing up in a country, is

C c 4 therefore

therefore not to be calculated by the number of inhabitants, but by the number whofe
minds receive that degree of cultivation neceffary to call forth their latent powers.

On the fuppofition, that one kingdom
contains eight millions of inhabitants, and
another triple the number, many more
men of original genius, and great eminence
in every art and fcience, may, from the circumftances above mentioned, be expected
to appear in the firft than in the fecond. In
Great Britain, for example, almoft all the
natives may be included in the calculation ;
but in the other countries which I have
mentioned, the peafantry, who form the
moft numerous clafs, muft be ftruck out.

LETTER XCIV.

Vienna.

WHETHER it is owing to the example of the Emprefs, or to what other caufe, I fhall not take upon me to decide; but there certainly appears a warmer and more general attachment to religion in Vienna, than in any other great town in Germany: There is alfo a greater appearance of fatisfaction and happinefs here than in many other cities, where religious impreffions are more feeble and lefs prevalent: It is not improbable, that the latter may be a confequence of the former.

Irreligion and fcepticifm, exclufive of the bad effects they may have on the

morals

morals or future deftiny of men, impair
even their temporal happinefs, by ob-
fcuring thofe hopes, which, in fome fituations, are their only confolation. In
whatever fuperior point of view thofe men
may confider themfelves, who deride the
opinions which their fellow-citizens hold
facred, this vanity is often overbalanced
by the irkfome doubts which obtrude on
their minds. Uncertainty with refpect to
the moft interefting of all fubjects, or a
fixed perfuafion of annihilation, are equally
infupportable to the greater part of mankind, who fooner or later endeavour to put
in a claim for that bright reverfion, which
religion has promifed to believers. If the
idea of annihilation has been fupported
without pain by a few philofophers, it is
the utmoft that can be faid; fuch a ftate
of mind can never be a fource of fatisfaction or pleafure. People of great fenfibility feldom endure it long; their fond
                                        defire

defire of immortality overturns every fabric which fcepticifm had attempted to
raife in their minds; they cannot abide
by a doctrine which plucks from the
heart a deeply-rooted hope, tears afunder
all thofe ties of humanity, affection,
friendfhip, and love, which it has been
the bufinefs of their lives to bind, and
which they expect will be eternal. Since
fenfibility renders the heart averfe to
fcepticifm, and inclinable to devotion,
we may naturally expect to find women
more devout than men; very few of that
delicate fex have been able to look with
ftedfaft eyes on a profpect, which terminates in a difmal blank; and thofe few,
who have had that degree of philofophical fortitude, have not been the moft
amiable of the fex.

None of my female acquaintance at
Vienna are in this uncomfortable ftate of
mind; but many of them have embroidered
fome

fome fanciful piece of fuperftition of their own upon the extenfive ground which the Roman Catholic faith affords. In a lady's houfe, a few days ago, I happened to take up a book which lay upon the table,—a fmall picture of the Virgin Mary on vellum fell from between the leaves; under the figure of the Virgin there was an infcription, which I tranflate literally:

" This is prefented by —— —— to her
" deareft friend —— ——, in token of the
" fincereft regard and affection; begging
" that as often as fhe beholds this figure of
" the bleffed Virgin, fhe may mix a fenti-
" ment of affection for her abfent friend,
" with the emotions of gratitude and ado-
" ration fhe feels for the Mother of Jefus."

The lady informed me, that it was ufual for intimate friends to fend fuch prefents to each other when they were about to fepa-rate, and when there was a probability of their being long afunder.

There

There feems to be fomething exceedingly ·
tender and pathetic in blending friendfhip
with religious fentiments, and thus, by a
kind of confecration, endeavouring to preferve the former from the effects of time and
abfence.—The perufal of this infcription recalled to my memory certain connections I
have at home, the impetuofity of which
recollection affected me beyond expreffion.

I remarked in this lady's houfe another
beautiful picture of the Virgin, ornamented
with a rich frame, and a filk curtain to preferve it from duft; I obferved that fhe never
looked at it but with an air of veneration
and love, nor paffed it when uncovered by
the curtain without a gentle bending of the
knee.—She told me, that this picture had
been long in the family, and had been always held in the higheft efteem; for that
both her mother and fhe owed fome of the
moft fortunate events of their lives to the
protection of the bleffed Virgin, and fhe
feemed not intirely free from a perfuafion,

that

that the attention of the Virgin was in some
degree retained by the good offices of this
identical picture. She declared, that the
confidence she had in the Virgin's goodnefs
and protection, was one of the greateft comforts she had in life—that to *her* she could,
without reftraint, open her heart, and pour
out her whole foul under every affliction,
and she never failed to find herself com-
forted and relieved by fuch effusions.

I obferved, that devout proteftants found
the fame confolation in addreffing the Almighty.

She faid—She could not comprehend how
that could be—for that God the Father was
fo great and awful, that her veneration was
mixed with fuch a degree of dread, as confounded all her ideas when she attempted
to approach him; but the bleffed Mary was
of fo mild, fo condefcending, and compaf-
fionate a character, that she could addrefs
her with more confidence.

She

She faid, fhe knew it was her duty to adore the Creator of the univerfe, and fhe fulfilled it to the beft of her power; but fhe could not diveft herfelf of a certain degree of reftraint in her devotions to Him, or even to her Saviour. But the bleffed Mary being herfelf a woman, and acquainted with all the weaknefs and delicacies of the fex, fhe could to *her* open her heart with a degree of freedom, which it was not poffible for her to ufe to any of the Perfons of the Holy Trinity.—Regardez fa phyfionomie, added fhe, pointing to the picture,—mon Dieu, qu'elle eft douce, qu'elle eft gracieufe!

Thefe fentiments, however contrary to the Proteftant tenets, and the maxims of philofophy, are not unnatural to the human heart.—Voltaire fays, That man has always fhewn an inclination to create God after his own image; this lady formed an idea of the bleffed Virgin from the reprefentation of the painter, as well as from the account

given of her in the Evangelifts; and her religion allowing the Mother of Chrift to be
an object of worſhip, ſhe naturally turned
the ardor of her devotion to her, whoſe power
ſhe imagined was ſufficient to protect her
votaries here, and procure them paradiſe
hereafter; and whoſe character ſhe thought,
in ſome particulars, ſympathiſed with her
own.

Some zealous Proteſtants may poſſibly be
ſhocked at this lady's theological notions:
however, as in other reſpects ſhe is a woman
of an excellent character, and obſerves the
moral precepts of Chriſtianity with as much
attention as if her creed had been purified
by Luther, and doubly refined by Calvin, it
is hoped they will not think it too great an
extenſion of charity to ſuppoſe that her
ſpeculative errors may be forgiven.

LETTER XCV.

Vienna.

THE preference which is given by individuals in Roman Catholic countries to particular Saints, proceeds sometimes from a suppofed connection between the characters of the Saints and the votaries. Men expect the greateft favour and indulgence from thofe who moft refemble themfelves, and naturally admire others for the qualities which they value moft in their own character.

A French officer of dragoons, being at Rome, went to view the famous ftatue of Mofes by Michael Angelo. The artift has conveyed into this mafter-piece, in the opinion of fome, all the dignity which a human form and human features are capable of receiving;

VOL. II.   D d   ceiving;

ceiving; he has endeavoured to give this
ſtatue a countenance worthy of the great le-
giſlator of the Jews, the favourite of Heaven,
who had converſed face to face with the
Deity. The officer happened to be acquainted with the hiſtory of Moſes, but he
laid no great ſtreſs on any of theſe circumſtances—he admired him much more on account of one adventure in which he imagined Moſes had acquitted himſelf like a
man of ſpirit, and as he himſelf would have
done——Voilà qui eſt terrible! voilà qui
eſt ſublime! cried he at ſight of the ſtatue—
and after a little pauſe he added, on voit là
un drôle qui a donné des coups de bâton en
ſon tems, et qui a tué ſon homme.

The crucifixes, and ſtatues, and pictures,
of Saints, with which Popiſh churches are
filled, were no doubt intended to awaken
devotion when it became drowſy, and to
excite in the mind gratitude and veneration
for the holy perſons they repreſent; but it
cannot be denied that the groſs imagina-
tions

tions of the generality of mankind are exceedingly prone to forget the originals, and transfer their adoration to the fenfelefs figures which they behold, and before which they kneel. So that whatever was the original defign, and whatever effects thofe ftatues and pictures have on the minds of calm, fenfible Roman Catholics, it is certain that they often are the objects of as complete idolatry as ever was practifed in Athens or Rome, before the ftatues of Jupiter or Apollo.

On what other principle do fuch multitudes flock from all the Roman Catholic countries in Europe to the fhrine of our Lady at Loretto? Any ftatue of the Virgin would ferve as effectually as that to recal her to the memory; and people may adore her as devoutly in their own parifh churches, as in the chapel at Loretto.—The pilgrims, therefore, muft be perfuaded that there is fome divine influence or intelligence in the

D d 2 ftatue

ftatue which is kept there; that it has a confcioufnefs 'of all the trouble they have taken, and the inconveniencies to which they have been expofed, by long journies, for the fole purpofe of kneeling before it, in preference to all other images.

It was probably on account of this tendency of the human mind, that the Jews were forbid to make unto themfelves any graven image. This indeed feems to have been the only method of fecuring that fuperftitious people from idolatry; and, notwithftanding the peremptory tenor of the commandment, neither the zeal nor remonftrances of their judges and prophets could always prevent their making idols, nor hinder their worfhipping them wherever they found them ready made.

Statues and pictures of Saints, which have been long in particular families, are generally kept with great care and attention; the proprietors often have the fame kind of attachment

ment to them, that the ancient heathens had to their Dii Penates.—They are confidered as tutelary and domeftic divinities, from whom the family expect protection. When a feries of unfortunate events happens in a family, it fometimes creates a fufpicion that the family ftatues have loft their influence. This alfo is a very ancient fentiment. Suetonius informs us, that the fleet of Auguftus having been difperfed by a ftorm, and many of the fhips loft, the Emperor gave orders that the ftatue of Neptune fhould not be carried in proceffion with thofe of the other Gods, from an opinion that the God of the Sea was unwilling or unable to protect his navy; and in either cafe he deemed him not worthy of any public mark of diftinction.

The genuine tenets of the Roman Catholic church certainly do not authorife any of the fuperftitions above-mentioned, which are generally confined to the credulous and illiterate in the lower ranks of

life.

life.—Yet inſtances are ſometimes to be met
with in a higher ſphere. A Frenchman in
a creditable way of life had a ſmall figure
of our Saviour on the Crofs, of very curious workmanſhip; he offered it for ſale
to an Engliſh gentleman of my acquaintance: after expatiating on the excellency
of the workmanſhip, he told him that he
had long kept this crucifix with the moſt
pious care, that he had always addreſſed it
in his private devotion, and that in return
he had expected ſome degree of protection
and favour; inſtead of which he had of
late been remarkably unfortunate : that all
the tickets he had in the lottery had proved
blanks: and having had a great ſhare in
the cargo of a ſhip coming from the Weſt-
Indies, he had recommended it in the moſt
fervent manner in his prayers to the crucifix ; and, that he might give no offence by
any appearance of want of faith, he had
not inſured the goods—notwithſtanding all
which the veſſel had been ſhipwrecked,
and

and the cargo totally loft, though the failors, in whofe prefervation he had no concern, had been all faved—Enfin, Monfieur, cried he, with an accent of indignation mingled with regret, and raifing his fhoulders above his ears, Enfin, Monfieur, il m'a manqué, et je vends mon Chrift.

Happy for Chriftians of every denomination, could they abide by the plain, rational, benevolent precepts of the Chriftian religion; rejecting all the conceits of fuperftition, which never fail to deform its original beauty, and to corrupt its intrinfic purity!

D d 4

LETTER XCVI.

Vienna.

OUR difputes with the colonies have been a prevailing topic of converfation wherever we have been fince we left England. The warmth with which this fubject is handled, increafes every day. At prefent, the inhabitants of the continent feem as impatient as thofe of Great Britain, for news from the other fide of the Atlantic; but with this difference, that here they are all of one mind:—all praying for fuccefs to the Americans, and rejoicing in every piece of bad fortune which happens to our army.

That the French fhould be pleafed with commotions which muft diftrefs and weaken Great Britain, and may transfer to them an

equal

equal right to every advantage we gained by the laſt war, is not ſurpriſing; but why the inhabitants of every other country ſhould take part againſt England, and become partizans of America, is not ſo apparent.

I ſhould forgive them, and even join in ſentiment with them, as far as my regard for the honour and happineſs of my country would permit, if this proceeded from an attachment to liberty, and a generous partiality for men who repel oppreſſion, and ſtruggle for independency.—But this is not the caſe.—Thoſe who can reap no poſſible advantage from the revolt of America; thoſe who have not an idea of civil liberty, and would even be ſorry to ſee it eſtabliſhed in their own country; thoſe who have no other knowledge of the diſpute, than that it is ruining England; all join as allies to the Americans, not from love to them, but evidently from diſlike to us.

When

When I firſt obſerved this hoſtile diſpoſition, I thought it might proceed from their being offended at that preference which the Engliſh give to their own country and countrymen, above all others: but this conceit we have in common with every other nation on the globe, all of whom cheriſh the ſame favourable opinion of themſelves. It aſſuredly prevails in France in an eminent degree.—There is hardly one ſceptic or unbeliever in the whole nation.—It is the univerſal creed, that France is the fineſt country in the world; the French the moſt ingenious and moſt amiable people, excelling in all the arts of peace and war; and that Paris is the capital of politeneſs, and the centre of learning, genius, and taſte.

This ſatisfaction at the misfortunes of Great Britain cannot therefore ariſe from a cauſe which is applicable to every other country. It may indeed, in ſome meaſure, fure, proceed from envy of the riches, and jealoufy of the power, of the Englifh nation; but, I believe, ftill more from our taking no trouble to conciliate the affections of foreigners, and to diminifh that envy and ill-will which great profperity often creates. The French, though perhaps the vaineft people on earth of their own advantages, have fome degree of confideration for the feelings and felf-love of their neighbours. A Frenchman endeavours to draw from them an acknowledgment of the fuperiority of his country, by making an elogium on whatever is excellent in theirs. But we are apt to build our panegyric of Old England, on the ruin and wretchednefs of all other countries. —Italy is too hot, the inns miferable, and the whole country fwarms with monks and other vermin.—In France, the people are flaves and coxcombs, the mufic execrable; —they boil their meat to rags, and there is no porter, and very little ftrong ale, in the country.

country.—In Germany, fome of their Princes have little more to fpend than an Englifh gentleman:—They ufe ftoves inftead of
grates;—they eat four crout, and fpeak
High Dutch.—The Danes and Swedes are
reminded, that they are rather at too great
a diftance from the equator; and many fly
hints are given concerning the inconveniencies of a cold climate.—Of all things,
I fhould think it moft prudent to be filent
on this laft topic, as fo many paltry ftates
will take precedency of Old England, whenever it is the eftablifhed etiquette that rank
fhall be determined by climate.

But this confideration has no effect on
my honeft friend John Bull. When he is
in a choleric humour, he will not fpare his
beft friends and neareft neighbours, even
when he has moft need of their affiftance,
and when thofe at a diftance feem to have
plotted his ruin.—If his own fifter Peg
fhould fhow a difpofition to forget old
fquabbles,

fquabbles, to live in friendfhip with her
brother, and fhould declare that all who
renounced his friendfhip were her enemies,
and refolve to conquer by his fide, or if that
fhould fail, to die hard along with him—
No! d—n ye, fays John, none of your
coaxing:—You be d—d! you are farther
North than I—Keep your diftance.———
And fo he falls a pelting Peg with her own
fnow-balls; and then turning from her, he
attacks Lewis Baboon, Lord Strut, Lord
Peter, and dafhes their foup maigre, olio's,
and maccaroni, full in their teeth.

But to drop allegory; the univerfal fatif-
faction which appears all over Europe, at
the idea of England's being ftript of her
colonies, certainly does not intirely origi-
nate from political fentiments; but in a
great degree from that referve which keeps
Englifhmen from cultivating the friendfhip
of foreigners; that pride which hinders
them from ftooping to humour prejudices;
that

S

that indifference which makes them difregard the approbation of others, and betray the contempt they are too ready to entertain for cuftoms or fentiments different from their own.

These are things not eafily forgiven, and for which no fuperiority of genius, magnanimity, or integrity, can compenfate. The fame caufes which have made foreigners take part againft us in the difpute with America, induce thofe of them who are rich, and can fpend their revenues out of their own country, to prefer France to England for that purpofe. The difference between London and Paris in point of climate is very fmall. The winter amufements of the former are more magnificent; and perhaps every conveniency, and moft of the luxuries of life are to be found there in greater perfection. During the fummer months, by fuperior fkill in agriculture and a better tafte in gardening, England difplays

                                                    fuch

such scenes of cultivation, of verdure and fertility, as no country on earth can equal. To these are added the blessings of liberty; yet few or no foreigners reside in England, except those she maintains entirely at her own expence; all the wealthy, after a short visit to London, returning to spend their fortunes at Paris.

Exclusive of pecuniary advantages, it flatters the natural vanity of the French to find their society preferred to that of all other people, and particularly to that of their proud rivals.—Let them enjoy this advantage; let them draw to their capital the idle, the dissipated, and the effeminate of every country in Europe :—but for heaven's sake, do you and your friends in parliament fall on some measure to prevent them from engaging the affections of our industrious brethren of America.

Such an event would be attended with severe consequences to Great Britain, and probably

probably to America. There are, however, so many repelling points in the American and French characters, that I cannot imagine the adhesion between them could be of long duration, should it take place.

You may naturally suppose, from some things in this letter, that the people here are in a particular manner inveterate against England, in her dispute with America. But in reality this is not the case: for although in general they favour America, I have not seen so much moderation on that question any where as at Vienna. The Emperor, when some person asked which side he favoured, replied very ingeniously, Je suis par métier royaliste.

I wish those of our countrymen, who by your account seem to be carrying their zeal for America too far, would remember qu'ils sont par naissance Anglois.

Just as I was concluding the above I received yours, informing me that your young friend

friend was in a fhort time to fet out on the ufual tour through Europe. I fhall take another opportunity of writing to him on the fubject you defire; at prefent I muft confine myfelf to the few following hints.

I hope he will always remember that virtue and good fenfe are not confined to any particular place, and that one end of travelling is to free the mind from vulgar prejudices—he ought therefore to form connections, and live on a focial footing with the inhabitants of the different countries through which he paffes; let him at leaft feem pleafed while he remains among them; this is the moft effectual method of making them pleafed with him, and of his accomplifhing every object he can have in vifiting their country.

There are inftances of Englifhmen, who, while on their travels, fhock foreigners by an oftentatious preference of England to all the reft of the world, and ridicule the manners, cuftoms, and opinions of every other nation; yet on their return to their own country, immediately affume foreign manners, and continue during the remainder of their lives to exprefs the higheft contempt for every thing that is Englifh.——— I hope he will entirely avoid fuch perverfe and ridiculous affectation.

The tafte for letters which he has acquired at the univerfity, I dare fay will not be diminifhed on claffic ground, or his mind be diverted, by a frivolous enthufiafm for mufic, or any other paffion, from the manly ftudies and purfuits which become an Englifh gentleman.

As he regards the confidence of his friends, the prefervation of his character, and the tranquillity of his mind, let no example, however high, lead him into the practice of deep play. By avoiding gaming he will fecure one kind of independence,

I   and

and at the fame time keep poffeffion of another, by continuing the habit of ftudy, till the acquifition of knowledge has become one of his moft pleafing amufements.—Unlike thofe wretched mortals, who, to drag through the dreary hours of life, are continually obliged to have recourfe to the affiftance of others, this fortunate turn of mind will add to his own happinefs, while it renders him more ufeful to, and lefs dependent on, fociety.

The preceding fermon, if you think proper, you may deliver to the young traveller, with my beft wifhes.

Having delayed our journey feveral weeks longer than was intended, merely from a reluctance of leaving a place which we have found fo very agreeable, we have at length determined to fet out for Italy—and are to go by the Duchies of Stiria and Carinthia, which is a fhorter route than that by the Tirol. As the time we are to remain at

Vienna

Vienna will be entirely employed in the neceffary arrangements for the journey, and
the painful ceremony of taking leave of
friends, you will not hear again from me
till we arrive at Venice.——Mean while, I
am, &c.

T H E   E N D.

www.ingramcontent.com/pod-product-compliance
Lightning Source LLC
Chambersburg PA
CBHW030955110726
47900CB00004B/1278